Glory Days

elizabeth laing

Glory Days

real-life answers for teens

DPI

DISCIPLESHIP
PUBLICATIONS
INTERNATIONAL

Glory Days
©1999 by Discipleship Publications International
One Merrill Street, Woburn, MA 01801

All Scripture quotations, unless indicated, are taken from
the NEW INTERNATIONAL VERSION.
Copyright ©1973, 1978, 1984 by the International Bible Society.
Used by permission of Zondervan Publishing House.
All rights reserved.

The "NIV" and "New International Version" trademarks
are registered in the United States Patent Trademark Office
by the International Bible Society.
Use of either trademark requires the permission of
the International Bible Society.

Printed in the United States of America

Book design: Chris Costello
Images ©1999, PhotoDisc, Inc.

ISBN: 1-57782-060-6

To my parents,
Sam and Geri Laing:

I don't know why God allowed me to
be your daughter; I only know that words could
never express the depth of my gratitude or
the enormity of my love for you.
It is I who am proud of you.

Contents

Foreword

The teen years. Maddening, exhilarating, miserable, glass-shattering, metal-bending, ear-splitting, tear-filled, reckless...and forever hopeful. Most people my age look back on that time in our lives with an odd mixture of relief and fear. How did we ever survive? We blitzed through those years studying, practicing sports, dancing, playing, talking, making friends, breaking up. Some of us cheated death again and again, getting involved with drugs, fast cars and the kind of people our moms called "disreputable." We played; our parents prayed. Those years were a time of great expectations, mercurial dreams and unanswered questions: *Who am I, anyway? What does God want from me? How do I know?*

I almost backed out of doing this when Elizabeth said she wanted me to write about *my* teen years. Those were the worst of my life. The only good thing I can say is that I became a disciple before my nineteenth birthday. The bad thing is...that was too late. Too late for me to avoid the devastating consequences of heart-breaking sins I've had to live with to this day. Too late to dodge the mistakes, which have left scars in my life forever. But not too late for the passion I felt to thank God for his forgiveness, the gratitude that motivates me every day, even now as I approach the ripe old age of forty-two.

I grew up in a divided home. My mother came from a very religious family and raised me to believe in God. My father came from a different world and raised me to believe in ME. When I was young, I yearned for my mother's God. But at fifteen I began a trip into Hell, involving all the bad the '70s had to offer. By the time I was eighteen

I knew just enough about God and the Bible to think that I'd ruined my life. Then I turned to the Lord like I never knew you could. A disciple reached out to me and taught me that you can't ruin a life beyond God's ability to repair it. I became a Christian at eighteen and the gratitude I felt, thankfulness to be forgiven for all the garbage and junk I'd done, has propelled me for the last twenty-three years.

My passion in life is to find and train young, sold-out-for-Jesus, talented women, women zealous for the mission God gave all his disciples and who don't want to wait until they're twenty to lead. Women like Anna Leatherwood and Carla Gehl who were appointed as women's ministry leaders when they were nineteen. Women who don't lower the standard for leadership but raise it in their youth by proving that being young doesn't mean being immature, selfish or foolish, if you walk in the Spirit. Women who know that if you stay close to God, the sky is the only limit to your dreams. Women like Cinnamon Conner who was asked to lead the women of the Manhattan region of the New York church, a ministry with 1,500 disciples—larger than 95 percent of all the churches in our fellowship—*when she was 21 years old*.

Elizabeth Laing epitomizes this kind of woman. I'll never forget hearing her speak at a women's day when she was a senior in high school. I cried. I dreamed. I hoped for my two daughters.

With our first generation of kingdom kids in the modern movement reaching adulthood, we see so clearly God's plan for teens. He provides the answers to all the maddening questions and a standard that never changes, in spite of confusing emotions and shifting circumstances. Kids in the kingdom have something to level them. They can be certain that everything will turn out okay, even if they don't know exactly how God will work it out.

Elizabeth is one of those kingdom kids whom I've known since she was tiny. Even though she was raised in a great home with loving and supportive Christian parents, she fought her own battles with authority, pride and emotionalism. And now she's written about those skirmishes and heartaches in a way that's brilliant, generous and insightful beyond her years.

Glory Days is a practical, day-to-day survival guide for teenagers and deals candidly with tough issues. Elizabeth unselfishly shares her life and humbly demonstrates how faith and perseverance will lead teens to victory in the Lord. An inspiration to parents and a gift to our kids, I'm sure this is just the first of many books by a new, young author and leader in God's kingdom.

The real introduction to this book was published several years ago by Elizabeth's parents, Sam and Geri Laing. *Raising Awesome Kids in Troubled Times* is an invaluable reference book for all disciples. For years now Sam and Geri have been leading the way in teaching all of us how to get our kids to heaven. *Glory Days* is the sequel to that book, and the fruit of an entire family devoted to the Lord.

—Lisa Johnson
February 1999

Acknowledgments

There are countless people to thank for their help in writing this book. To my parents I owe more than I can ever say. I never would have made it into the kingdom, much less through my high school years, without their love. They have always been my biggest fans in all I have done, especially in my writing endeavors. It was at their suggestion that I even considered writing this book in the first place.

To my fiancé Kevin Thompson, thank you for believing in me, praying for me and supporting me so selflessly throughout this entire process.

Special thanks also to my brothers and sister for their prayers during the past year.

I want to thank the staff of Triangle Church, especially Casto and Angie Fernandez, for their encouragement as well.

To Tracy MacLachlan, thank you so much for all the countless ways you have helped me, not only with this project, but with my life too.

I want to especially thank Christina Askounis, of the Duke University writing program, who worked with me on this book as an independent study project. Her encouragement, suggestions and thoughtful critiques were invaluable.

In a special way I want to thank Bob and Pat Gempel, Kyle and Marcy Lindenmuth, Eddie and Roxanne Armes and all who have worked with the HOPE Youth Corps, sponsored by HOPE *worldwide*, during the past few years. You may never know all the good your tireless efforts have wrought in so many lives, but thank you with all of my heart. The Youth Corps has been a defining experience throughout my teen and college years, and I cannot even express all that it has done for me and so many others. I have had the opportunity to travel around the US and other nations of the world, working with groups of young people from all over the kingdom to meet the needs of the poor—building lifelong friendships along the way.

To Tom and Sheila Jones, Chris Costello, Kim Hanson, Lisa Morris and the entire DPI staff, thank you for all that you have done for me, my family and God's kingdom. I deeply appreciate the opportunity to write this book, and all of your efforts throughout the process. Thank you for all that you have done to keep the kingdom healthy, Biblically sound and unified, and for your concern for even its youngest members.

And to all those I cannot name here who befriended, discipled and loved me through my teen years, I owe you my undying gratitude.

—Elizabeth Laing
Durham, North Carolina
January 1999

Introduction

And we, who with unveiled faces all reflect the
Lord's glory, are being transformed into his
likeness with ever-increasing glory, which comes
from the Lord, who is the Spirit.

2 CORINTHIANS 3:18

My life began when I was fourteen years old. I remember the day
and the moment so clearly: stepping down into the water, legs shak-
ing incessantly—half from excitement and half from cold. I was vaguely
aware of the hundreds of eyes staring at me, but the only ones I
really saw were the soft, teary ones of my father as he helped me into
the baptistery. I remember the fluttery feeling in my heart and the
new-found conviction that echoed in my voice as I slowly and em-
phatically spoke the three short words that have since defined my
life: *"Jesus is Lord."*

I grew up always knowing about God, and as a child, I loved him
deeply. But as I grew older, somehow my heart changed. I first studied the Bible to become a Christian when I was thirteen, but was too
immature and too prideful to face my own sin. I wanted to pretend I
did not know how serious my sin really was, and to go on living the
carefree, guilt-free life of a child. And so I did—but not really. Over
the next eight months, I threw myself fully into accomplishing my
own selfish goals, and my heart hardened more and more as I did so.
I can still feel the icy tentacles of arrogance and self-satisfaction that
gradually coiled around my heart, strangling it. I remember the dead-
ness of apathy that hardened into concrete within me. I could feel it
weighing me down, stifling me.

I heard the word of God preached at least three times a week and read it on my own every day but did not allow its powerful message to pierce my armor. I knew I could not really follow God because someone else had taken his place: Her name was Elizabeth Laing. She prided herself on being righteous and thought she could be a good person without God's help. She cared only about success. She wanted to have the very best grades, the most awards, the greatest recognition of anyone around her—at whatever cost. She wanted to be close to people, but competitiveness, jealousy and insecurity kept everyone away. At the same time she was haunted by oppressive guilt, and although at times she really wanted to change, she was terrified of facing who she had become.

It was finally a talk with my parents, and then with God, that changed me. My parents sat me down and challenged my sin, showing me clearly who I had become—and who I would be in a short time if I did not make some radical decisions. Although I was saddened by their words, my hard heart did not begin to soften until I begged God to change me and discovered this passage:

> "I revealed myself to those
>   who did not ask for me;
> I was found by those who did not seek me.
> To a nation that did not call on my name,
>   I said, 'Here am I, here am I.'
> All day long I have held out my hands
>   to an obstinate people,
> who walk in ways not good,
>   pursuing their own imaginations—
> a people who provoke me
>   to my very face...

who say, 'Keep away; don't come near me,
for I am too sacred for you!'" (Isaiah 65:1-3, 5)

When I finally realized that during my whole life God had eagerly sought a close relationship with me, even as I had deliberately, cruelly pushed him away, my heart softened and broke. I begged God for a new heart, repented, and was baptized the next day, on April 26, 1991.

I entered high school five months later with a completely new purpose: to win as many as possible for God. I still remember the eagerness I felt on the first day of my freshman year and my determination to have a great impact for God. The next four years were quite a ride—they were by far my most fun and thrilling years thus far, yet at the same time they were also the most emotional and challenging.

My freshman year was in many ways the most difficult. I was a brand new Christian, and I held myself to a standard so high no one could meet it. Even though my sins were forgiven, guilt dogged me constantly. I would not embrace God's grace and forgiveness. I felt that my sins were more awful and somehow more weird than other people's, and this belief left me feeling alone, isolated—even from other disciples. My loneliness was not helped by the fact that I was the only disciple at my high school and that I was also racially in the minority at my school. In the back of my mind I always felt different from other people, and although I had some friends and even served as our class president, I never thought people liked me all that much.

Over the next three years, God provided the people, circumstances and maturity I needed to help me start moving past my guilt and loneliness. My family moved several times, and I ended up attending three high schools in three different states. Our move to New Jersey right before my sophomore year was just what I needed: a chance to start over in a new school and in a new ministry, where no one thought of me as the old quiet, insecure, guilted-out Elizabeth. I formed close friendships for the first time in many years and rapidly grew in confidence and happiness.

But before the school year had even ended, my family moved again, this time to North Carolina. That move was one of the hardest things I had ever faced—I had been happy for the first time in several years, and we were leaving, going to a much smaller church in which I would be the entire teen ministry. I recognized then that God was using the move to refine me, but that fact became even more evident as time has passed. This move forced me to rely on God as never before and drew me out of the secure, comfortable spirituality I had found by having a strong group of teen disciples around me. Although it was tremendously challenging to start over again and to continue to grow on my own, I believe God honored my decision to be faithful and happy in our new home. He blessed me more in the last two years of high school in North Carolina than I had ever thought possible.

As graduation approached, I remember that so many around me were thrilled to finally be escaping high school (and their parents!). Although I was excited about going to college, I did not share their sentiments—I was sad to leave! I loved high school and hated to see such a wonderful era of my life come to an end. I loved all of the football and basketball games, cross-country practices, club meetings, pell-mell dashes to Wendy's at lunch time, and yes, I even loved the classes and study sessions with friends (Don't put the book down and run away screaming—you haven't even finished the introduction yet!). But most of all I loved all the great memories I had forged with the friends God had brought into my life during high school, both in the church and at school.

As graduation neared, I reflected back on the previous four years and realized that I had become a completely different person in that time. God had used high school to transform me from an immature, guilty, moody girl into a young woman who was far more confident, happy and spiritually mature. I still had (and have) innumerable areas to grow in, but I left high school with the rewarding knowledge that God had changed me and used me powerfully, in spite of my struggles!

I write all these things because I really want you to know me before you read this book. I do not claim to have had a perfect high school experience or to have been a perfect disciple—just keep reading, and you'll hear plenty about my abundant weaknesses! I only hope that the lessons I learned and convictions I developed will be of some help to you. High school and adolescence can be one of the most challenging and confusing periods of our lives, especially if we do not handle them in a godly way. I keenly felt every difficulty during those years of my life—and analyzed them backward and forward. I hope that many will relate to my sometimes irrational or borderline bizarre feelings and that my over-analyzing personality will finally prove useful! I attempt to provide a practical approach to many of the big issues that teens, and teen Christians in particular, face on a daily basis. We will look at everything from confidence to dating to relationships with parents.

It is also my hope that parents of teens will read this book to help them understand the way their teens' minds and emotions work. I remember how difficult it was at times for my parents to understand why I thought or felt certain ways, and they had to deal with me differently than they ever had before. Truthfully, most of this book is simply me restating all the things my parents taught me in high school about myself, my emotions and God.

Many times when adult disciples find out that I became a disciple in the eighth grade and stayed faithful and strong throughout my high school years, their eyes widen in amazement. Many say, "I respect you so much. I *never* could have done that!" They act as if it is impossible to be a faithful disciple during the teen years. It is time to challenge that fallacy and prove it wrong with our lives! Teens can not only be baptized, but they can grow into strong, confident and effective disciples.

Those of us who have heard God's word at a young age are absolutely the most blessed people alive! We will be spared so much sin, disappointment and heartache because of our godly lifestyles. Let us follow the examples of those in the Bible who first grew to love God in their adolescence and who only grew stronger as the years went by— people like David, Esther, Joseph, Joshua and Mary. Let us prove by our own examples that the teen years need not be a time of drudgery, disappointment or defeat. Let us decide to become strong men and women of God who stride through the teen years victoriously, and for whom the days of youth are indeed *glory days*.

1. Confidence

For you have been my hope,
O Sovereign Lord,
my confidence since my youth.
PSALM 71:5

He was the last person you would have expected to write such a poem. His was the life most high school students dream about having. As a tremendous athlete, top-notch student and outstanding performer, he was probably the most well known, respected and popular guy in his school. Everyone loved him: teachers and students, both guys and girls. As a freshman, he had already been dating the homecoming queen and partying with the cool crowd. By his junior year he was the talk of the town—the athlete being recruited by impressive colleges.

He should have been happy and completely confident, but his self-assurance was merely a facade. Haunted by insecurity and guilt, and having no one with whom he could talk honestly, he finally confessed his true feelings in this poem:

> *Hangin' out in school*
> *Tripping out with all the guys*
> *I want to be the one that they all know*
>
> *Going to the parties*
> *And being on the top*
> *There's no security with friends that come and go*

I got respect from town
    They think I'm living right
But my act is merely put on for them to see

You'd think my life is on a high
    But inside I feel low
I know that God's the only one
        that knows me...

Although he enjoyed high school and had many friends, insecurity nagged at him constantly, sometimes subtly, but it was always there. He thought the only way he could feel confident and happy was by remaining popular and successful.

In the end, his desire to be well-liked led him to compromise many of his convictions. He did things he knew were wrong because he wanted so badly to gain confidence through others' approval. Thankfully, he became a disciple several months after writing this poem. Although he has now become a powerful man of God, he still regrets some of the decisions he made because of his insecurity.

I am convinced that the biggest struggle teenagers face in their high school years is not rebellion, drug use or premarital sex: It is the battle with insecurity. It plagues us as our ever-present nemesis even after we become disciples. Unless each of us conquers our insecurities, they will eventually destroy our self-esteem, steal our joy and even lead us to do the things we swore we would never do.

I faced many challenges in high school, but the struggle to be confident was by far the most difficult and pervasive one. I attended three different high schools. I felt surrounded at each one by kids who were cooler than me, smarter than me, better dressed than me, more athletic than me—you name it. For a while I thought I was the only one who felt that way. As I grew more spiritual, I began to see through the confident masks people wore and finally realized the simplest yet most profound truth about high school: *Everyone is insecure.* It makes no difference whether they are homecoming queens, valedictorians or head cheer-leaders—every teenager battles the same ferocious, paralyzing demon of insecurity.

The *only* way to gain true, lasting confidence is through a relationship with God. We may have to fight for confidence every day, or even every hour, but with God we can attain it. We can tie Satan's hands and become victorious, confident, fruitful men and women of God. As true Christians, we have every reason to be the most confident people in our schools. I am convinced of that now, but it took a great deal of work to forge that belief. I spent many a quiet time in high school reminding myself of all the Bibli-cal reasons I have to be confident. Once I started to fight insecurity spiri-tually and to base my confidence in God, my whole perception of myself and the people around me changed.

The key to becoming truly confident lies in gaining a godly under-standing in two areas: First, we must understand who God is, and second we must grasp who we are as his children.

Who God Is

The God we serve is loving, merciful and compassionate to a level we cannot even comprehend. Teenagers seem to have a particularly difficult time grasping God's love and grace; many tend to be so negative and feel so condemned.

The fear of messing up and making God angry dogged me constantly throughout my teen years. I never could feel absolutely sure that I was going to heaven. I was terrified that if I had not already sinned one too many times, I was definitely teetering on the verge. I know that I am not the only one who felt that way—in fact I'd guess that most teen Christians experience similar feelings. It's no wonder we're insecure! If we lack confidence in our relationship with God, then we also lack it in every other area of our lives: in our talents and abilities, with our friends and in our evangelism.

For a long time, even though I read all the great promises in the Bible and saw what a loving God I served, I still felt that all his blessings and love were directed only at perfect people, not me. Well, that feeling was simply not true! God loves us and wants to be close to us regardless of our flaws and sins. I finally had to decide to ignore my emotions on this one and to believe the Bible instead. I read the same verses over and over again until they started sinking in and changing the way I felt.

Psalm 103 has been a favorite of mine since high school. I read it often to remind me of who God is and how he feels about me—and you, too!

> The Lord is compassionate and gracious,
>   slow to anger, abounding in love.
> He will not always accuse,
>   nor will he harbor his anger forever;
> he does not treat us as our sins deserve
>   or repay us according to our iniquities.
> For as high as the heavens are above the earth,
>   so great is his love for those who fear him;
> as far as the east is from the west,
>   so far has he removed our transgressions
>   from us.

> **As a father has compassion on his children,
> so the Lord has compassion on those who
> fear him. (Psalm 103:8-13)**

Even now, as I read these words, I can feel the love of God wash over me and envelop me in a blanket of security. We serve a compassionate God, a God so caring that he cannot possibly give all of his love away! He does not get ticked off and kick us out of the kingdom every time we sin. He is *slow* to anger. As our spiritual Father, he picks us up when we fall, holds our hands and helps us to start over again. He is so merciful that he doesn't even remember our sins once he has forgiven us!

Do you realize that God is your Father, your Dad? You are "Daddy's little boy or girl"! It doesn't matter to him that you aren't perfect and that you mess up—he thinks you're wonderful just because you're his son or daughter. It took me a long time to really understand what it means to be God's child. I'm still learning. I have been blessed with a great relationship with my earthly father and having that relationship has helped me to understand more about how God, my spiritual Father, feels about me.

My dad is incredibly patient with me. I feel so secure in his love. He doesn't just love me; he likes me! The Bible says in Zephaniah 3:17 that God delights in his children. Have you ever watched a father with his newborn baby? Gazing at her with adoration in his eyes, he proclaims her the most perfect child ever born. He even makes a fool out of himself for her—crinkling his face, sticking out his tongue, and imitating her gurgles and baby talk—all just to see her tiny face light up with a smile.

Believe it or not, God feels the same way about us. He does special things for us every day, just hoping to make us smile or laugh. His favorite thing to do is to watch us. He thinks we're adorable, flaws and all. Do you know the little quirks you have that drive your friends crazy? God even loves those things about you!

My dad expects me to mess up sometimes, and he doesn't hold grudges when I do. When I apologize, he gives me a huge hug, extends to me his complete forgiveness, and then we both move on. Sometimes he corrects me, disciplines me and occasionally rebukes me, but those times are not the focus of our relationship. Mostly we just love being together and having fun.

I now realize that my relationship with God should work in much the same way. I used to talk to God only about my sin and what a horrible person I was, but I've now realized that God doesn't want that kind of a relationship with me. He just wants to enjoy hanging out with me and becoming closer to me.

Those of you who have a close relationship with your earthly father can use that relationship to help you understand what it means to be close to God. Others of you may not be close to your dad. He may be a poor example of what a father should be like—or maybe you don't even know him. In that case it is especially important for you to allow God to be your father. You may need to radically change your view of what a father is like. Soak in all the verses you can about God as a father, and watch some of the Christian fathers in your church with their children to help you to have a Biblical perspective.

Above all, realize that God's opinion of us is the only one that really matters. The Creator of the universe thinks we're awesome—so why in the world would we spend our time worrying about the opinions of some high school kids? We already have the approval of the only One who really matters!

Who We Are

Once you understand who God is and how he feels about you, you must understand who you are as his son or daughter. There are incredible blessings and privileges that come along with this title. Do you realize that you now have your own personal knight in shining armor? Just as the knights in the Middle Ages would protect and defend the honor of the women they loved, so we are under the protection of our God.

I still remember the night I first read the passage that became the theme for the rest of my years in high school, the verse that transformed the way I viewed myself. I was a sophomore and a newcomer to a snobby high school in northern New Jersey. Not surprisingly, insecurity was a big challenge for me that year. I was at a teen devotional one Friday night, and the speaker read this passage:

> But now, this is what the Lord says—
>   he who created you, O Jacob,
>   he who formed you, O Israel:
> "Fear not, for I have redeemed you;
>   I have summoned you by name;
>   you are mine.
> When you pass through the waters,
>   I will be with you;
> and when you pass through the rivers,
>   they will not sweep over you.
> When you walk through the fire,
>   you will not be burned;
>   the flames will not set you ablaze.
> For I am the Lord, your God,
>   the Holy One of Israel, your Savior;

> I give Egypt for your ransom,
>   Cush and Seba in your stead.
> Since you are precious and honored
>   in my sight,
>   and because I love you,
> I will give men in exchange for you,
>   and people in exchange for your life.
> Do not be afraid, for I am with you;
>   I will bring your children from the east
>   and gather you from the west."
>   (Isaiah 43:1-5)

As I listened to these promises, I suddenly began to realize how special I am as God's daughter. God selected each of us by name to belong to him. He could have selected anyone on earth, but he chose us! We are so special and so blessed to be God's chosen ones. As such, we are "precious and honored" in his sight. He respects and treasures us; as it says in Exodus 19:5, we are his "treasured possession."

When we go through tough situations at school or home, God is there with us, granting us victory and success. He doesn't claim that we will never face challenging times or difficult circumstances, but he does promise to be with us in the midst of those times. He never gives us more than we can handle (1 Corinthians 10:13-14), and he promises that we will somehow gain the victory in everything that we go through.

I always used to imagine, as I walked through the hallways, that God walked right beside me, holding my hand. I also used to imagine that Jesus, who the Bible says is our big brother (Hebrews 2:11), walked behind me, ready to defend me from anyone who dared to mess with his little sister! Talk about a confidence booster—I know it may sound a little crazy, but it sure helped me!

Another theme passage for me in high school (one I still cling to today) was Romans 8, especially verses 31 through 39:

> What, then, shall we say in response to this? If God is for us, who can be against us? He who did not spare his own Son, but gave him up for us all—how will he not also, along with him, graciously give us all things? Who will bring any charge against those whom God has chosen? It is God who justifies. Who is he that condemns? Christ Jesus, who died—more than that, who was raised to life—is at the right hand of God and is also interceding for us. Who shall separate us from the love of Christ? Shall trouble or hardship or persecution or famine or nakedness or danger or sword? As it is written:
>
> > "For your sake we face death all day long;
> > we are considered as sheep to be
> > slaughtered."
>
> No, in all these things we are more than conquerors through him who loved us. For I am convinced that neither death nor life, neither angels nor demons, neither the present nor the future, nor any powers, neither height nor depth, nor anything else in all creation, will be able to separate us from the love of God that is in Christ Jesus our Lord. (Romans 8:31-39)

We are truly so special to God, handpicked to be his adopted sons and daughters. And God doesn't make mistakes. Sometimes we can feel like the omniscient Creator must not realize how sinful we really are. We think that maybe his eyes were closed or his back was turned most of the times when we were sinning, so he just doesn't realize how bad we are; or maybe he meant to save our next-door neighbor, but got confused and accidentally sent salvation to our house instead. "Gabriel!" we imagine his furious voice thundering. "You read me the wrong address again! Do you realize who just received salvation?! It's that, that *awful* teen—the one who can't do anything right!"

Sounds ridiculous, right? But that's really how many of us think. Listen to yourself praying sometimes, and I'll bet you catch yourself trying to talk God *out* of loving you—repeatedly reminding him of what a horrible, sinful wretch you are, and how he should really find someone more righteous, someone who won't mess up as often as you do.

If you have ever done this, you are not alone. The Bible tells the stories of several men and women who, when called by God, attempted to warn him that he had made a mistake in choosing them. Look at the calling of Moses in Exodus 3 and 4, and of Gideon in Judges 6. Their responses sound just like ours do at times!

Moses felt compelled to remind the Almighty that, in case God had forgotten, he was a poor speaker and that God should find another guy to save Israel. Years later when God called Gideon, the young man reminded God that he belonged to the weakest clan around and that furthermore, he was the least member of his family.

God's response to both of these men is interesting. He didn't kick them out (although he may have felt like doing so!), but neither did he tell them all the wonderful qualities they possessed that led him to choose them. To both men, he simply responded, "I will be with you" (Exodus 3:12, Judges 6:16).

Who we are, what talents we have, and even how spiritual we are, do not matter to God nearly as much as we think. He knows we can accomplish great things with our lives and fulfill his goals for us, simply because he is with us! It is *his* power that makes us great, *his* strength that accomplishes his goals.

Stop questioning God for choosing you, and quit doubting yourself. None of us deserves to be saved, and none of us is talented enough to do all that God calls us to—by our own strength, that is. With God as our Commander, we can not only stand in the spiritual battle, but fight confidently until we attain a glorious victory!

Set Apart

We must realize that the honor of following God *does* set us apart from everyone else. Part of our confidence problem arises because we spend so much energy desperately trying to fit in and wishing we could be just like everyone else. But as disciples we must embrace the fact that we are different. The Bible talks often about how true Christians are strangers in the world, aliens who don't belong here. I don't know about you, but I do not want to look and act just like everyone else at school. I have no desire to be just another insecure girl who would do anything, no matter how sinful, in order to gain approval from my so-called friends. I would much rather stand out as a young woman of conviction who is confident enough to hold fast to my beliefs, thank you very much.

As I struggled to carry myself confidently and to share my faith boldly during my senior year, a friend helping me grow in Christ suggested that I read 2 Corinthians 5. This chapter changed the way I viewed myself then, and it still helps me to understand the difference between Christians and the world. We have been singled out and called for a very special purpose: to be God's ambassadors to the world (2 Corinthians 5:20). Do you realize what a privilege it is to have been selected to represent God? He has looked at thousands, millions, even billions of applicants, but he has chosen us to do it. Now we are the representatives of Christ on earth. Everywhere we walk, we represent Jesus. Because we are God's sons or daughters and ambassadors, each of us is the most important person at our school—more impressive than the cool crowd, more powerful than the student council president, stronger than the best athlete and more influential than the principal!

Practically Speaking

These truths did not sink in right away for me. I had to hear some of them over and over again until I really got them. I read Isaiah 43 and Romans 8 countless times until I really started believing they were true in my own life. Even now, I still have to remind myself of these convictions and lessons. Unfortunately, the battle to gain confidence will probably be a lifelong struggle for most of us. We must begin by deciding that we trust absolutely in God's love and promises, regardless of whether or not we *feel* that they are true. Our emotions, as powerful as they may feel, are not necessarily truth.

Developing strong friendships within the church can help increase your confidence. Although I was frequently the only disciple in my high schools, I felt much better about myself knowing that disciples at other schools were enduring the same challenges I was, and that they were praying for me. Even when I sometimes felt ignored or left out at school, it helped to know that I had close friends elsewhere who loved me no matter what I did. Their friendships even gave me the confidence to befriend some of the girls who intimidated me.

I also gained confidence at school by becoming part of some cool organizations on campus. I started running cross country during my junior year, and it was one of the best decisions I made in high school. It gave me a niche—a group to belong to. If you are not involved in anything at your school, I would strongly urge you to seek out a club or a team to join. Look for something that interests you and that corresponds with your talents. Being part of an organization quickly provides you with a group of potential friends and allows you to develop some of your abilities.

One word of caution: Be realistic in the activities you choose. As much as I might have wanted to be a cheerleader, I am inflexible, uncoordinated and somewhat rhythmically challenged! Attempting to be a cheerleader would have only depleted my confidence. Running cross country was a much more realistic endeavor for me and one in which I was able to succeed. I also worked on the school newspaper for two years, participated in student government and sang in the school chorus, among other things.

Although those activities were certainly fun, I always had to remember that being a disciple came first, especially when it came to my schedule. High school is an incredibly busy time of your life, and you may not have time to do everything you want to. For many the day starts as early as 5:30 or 6:00 am. Then there's six hours spent in class, immediately going to a club or activity, heading home in time for dinner, doing several hours of homework, heading straight to bed—and doing the same thing all over again the next day. (Even writing this down is exhausting!) None of us is Superman or Superwoman, so above all, be careful not to devote yourself to anything that will interfere with your commitment to God's kingdom.

An Attainable Victory

Confidence is not something that you gain right away, but you can attain it if you go about it in a godly manner. Each of us *must* conquer our insecurity if we want to be faithful and strong as disciples. If allowed to flourish in our hearts, it will ultimately make us miserable and lead us either to compromise as people-pleasers or to remain paralyzed as ineffective workers for God.

Although our heavenly Father is a patient God, he will not allow us to continue in either of these states. He expects his children to walk boldly and fearlessly, confident that he is with us every step of the way (Joshua 1:3). His command for us is the same as the one he gave to Joshua, the Israelite leader who succeeded Moses:

> "Be strong and courageous. Do not be terrified;
> do not be discouraged, for the Lord your God will be
> with you wherever you go." (Joshua 1:9)

Such a charge may seem daunting; it may seem frightening, discouraging and even impossible, but God would not give it to us unless he knew we could accomplish it. Let us all rise to his challenge and take steps toward becoming the confident disciples he wants us to be. Let us begin to lift our chins higher, walk with bolder steps and speak with the power that is ours through Christ. Only then will we become bold and unstoppable for God, fearing nothing, intimidated by no one and conquering Satan at every turn!

2. Relationship with God

Come near to God and he will come near to you.
JAMES 4:8

Have you ever fallen madly in love? Do you remember the feelings that washed over you? Just thinking about him was enough to send tingling air rushing through your body with every breath. You thought about him all the time—during classes, in the middle of the story your long-winded friend was telling you, any time you heard a romantic song on the radio, while doing your homework—all day long. He was all you wanted to talk about. You spent hours with your friends analyzing his every word and facial expression. Maybe you carried his picture around with you, and pulled it out several times a day. It was never a sacrifice or burden to spend time with him and you wanted to make him happy, no matter what.

Do you realize that a relationship with God should feel every bit as wonderful as being in love with another human being? Getting to know your Creator is just like falling in love, but few of us think of it in that way. For too many people, their relationship with God is not fun or exciting; rather, it is a burden to bear, a drudgery to endure. I have felt that way at times about getting to know God, and it seems that this pattern of thinking is shared by a large number of teenagers. If this describes you, then you need a major shift in the way you view God. Some of you may have allowed such feelings to make your efforts at getting to know him superficial and half-hearted; others may have avoided a relationship with him altogether.

Yet most of us, in our innermost hearts and selves, yearn for a relationship with God. We may not even realize that he is the relationship for which we are longing. We may think we are unhappy and unfulfilled because we need a boyfriend or girlfriend or closer friendships with others, or because we need to look more attractive, become more popular or successful, or make our lives more busy. But none of those things will truly fill the hole in our hearts that only God can fill. King Solomon realized this thousands of years ago: "[God] has...set eternity in the hearts of men" (Ecclesiastes 3:11).

So, how do you develop a close relationship with him? The answer is simple: Start by changing your image of God. Learn to view him as he intends you to, and this will help you figure out how to be close to him.

Understanding God

Many of us have never wanted to be close to God because we have held some very misguided notions about who he is. Let me start by clarifying for you some of the things that God is *not*:

- *God is not the great policeman in the sky.* Some of us picture him as a cop, secretly watching us from within his patrol car, hiding behind reflective sunglasses. He munches on a doughnut and waits for us to mess up so that he can switch on his flashing lights and pull us over. We think his sole purpose and joy in life lies in catching us in a mistake, and we live cowering in fear, constantly paranoid that we may do something wrong.

- *God is not a military dictator.* Others of us imagine that he struts around atop the clouds, smoking a cigar, yelling out commands and threatening horrible consequences if they are not obeyed immediately and unquestioningly. He makes up laws and rules that make absolutely no sense, just to make us miserable. Sometimes he even punishes us for no reason except to make a point or to prove his power.

- *God is not a Supreme Court judge.* Some of us envision him towering over the earth at a gigantic judge's desk, powdered white wig and all. He is aloof and impersonal and could care less about us as individuals. With a thundering bang of his gigantic gavel, he passes judgment on our lives, deaf to our pleas for mercy.

- *God is not a senile grandfather who sits in a rocking chair, smacking his toothless gums, and nodding and smiling at everything we do or say.* His favorite mottoes—when he can remember them—are, "Boys will be boys," and "Girls just want to have fun." Nothing we do could ever offend him (he is probably too blind and deaf to know about it anyway), and even if we break his rules, he is so kind that he will just let it pass.

These images may seem pretty ridiculous when we see them in print, but they accurately portray the various ways that many of us look at God. No wonder we don't want to be close to him! But if he is not any of these things, then who is he? What is he like? Many of us have a difficult time grasping the concept of being close to a spiritual being whom we cannot see, hear or touch. The cool thing about God is that he understands our limitations, so he describes himself in ways we can understand, comparing himself to several of the relationships we are most familiar with.

• *God is a father.* As discussed in the chapter on confidence, he is the perfect Dad. When we become true disciples, he adopts us as his sons and daughters. In Hosea 11:1-4, God describes his love for his children—the same love that he now lavishes upon us who follow him:

> When Israel was a child, I loved him....
> It was I who taught Ephraim to walk,
>   taking them by the arms;
> but they did not realize
>   it was I who healed them.
> I led them with cords of human kindness,
>   with ties of love;
> I lifted the yoke from their neck
>   and bent down to feed them. (Hosea 11:1-4)

There is something very special and unique about the relationship between a father and his daughter, particularly during the teenage years. As my high-school years progressed, I began to understand what an amazing man my dad is in a way I never had before. I found myself desperately wanting to be close to him—which, thankfully, we were. I needed his strength to stabilize me, his love to reassure me, his encouragement to make me confident. God wants so much to fulfill all of those roles in our lives—especially for those of us who do not have close relationships with our earthly fathers. Psalm 68:5 says that he is "a father to the fatherless."

• *God is like a husband or a boyfriend.* Isaiah 54:5-8 and 10 reads:

> For your Maker is your husband—
>   the Lord Almighty is his name—

the Holy One of Israel is your Redeemer;
   he is called the God of all the earth.
The Lord will call you back
   as if you were a wife deserted and distressed
      in spirit—
a wife who married young,
   only to be rejected," says your God.
"For a brief moment I abandoned you,
   but with deep compassion I will bring
      you back.
In a surge of anger
   I hid my face from you for a moment,
but with everlasting kindness
   I will have compassion on you,"
   says the Lord your Redeemer....
"Though the mountains be shaken
   and the hills be removed,
yet my unfailing love for you will not be shaken
   nor my covenant of peace be removed,"
   says the Lord, who has compassion on you.
   (Isaiah 54:5-8, 10)

In a sense, our Creator is in love with us, and his word is his love letter to us, his attempt to win our hearts. Do you realize that your Creator thinks you are a wonderful person? He adores everything about you, even your silly quirks.

- *God is a friend.* Exodus 33:11 describes the depth of closeness shared between Moses and the Almighty: "The LORD would speak to Moses face to face, as a man speaks with his friend." This is the kind of relationship God seeks with each of us. He longs to be our

very best friend—to be the one with whom we share our most intimate secrets, our innermost desires, dreams and emotions. He
wants to be the one we first run to when we need to talk; he wants
to laugh with us, hang out with us, cry with us.

These are relationships we *can* understand! Although we may not be
an expert at any of them, at least we have an idea of how they should
work. We can do this! We can learn what it means to be a devoted son or
daughter, a loving spouse—well, in our case, perhaps we better relate to
the idea of a boyfriend or girlfriend right now—okay, so we can learn
how to be a great boy- or girlfriend—and we can certainly become a
close friend.

Spend some time really thinking about this, because I guarantee it
will transform the way you relate to God. It will enable you to think of him
as someone real, someone you can be close to, and not as some nebulous
spirit floating around somewhere in space. Consider which of these relationships is the easiest for you. Are you close to your dad on earth? Is it
easy for you to be a good son or daughter? Or do you feel like you would
make a good boyfriend or girlfriend? Perhaps your strength lies in friendships with people. Figure out which one or ones are your strength(s), and
concentrate on replicating these strengths with God. Then think about
which of the three is more difficult for you, and work at turning your
weaknesses around.

Because I have always been close to my parents, I find it easiest to
think of myself as God's daughter. I have worked hard to gain a realistic
understanding of his love for me, and now that I feel more secure in his
love, it is much easier for me to feel confident, happy and secure. Friendships, on the other hand, have been an area I have had to learn a lot

about—and as a result, I have also had to train myself to be a friend to God. I am learning to be completely open with him about my feelings, to simply enjoy hanging out with him and having fun with him. Also, now that I am dating someone, I am learning what it means to be a "girlfriend" to God as well—how to be his biggest fan, how to serve him selflessly, how to commit myself to him even when things are difficult, how to enjoy being in love with him.

The 'Love Meter'

One good practical test of how close you are to God is the 1 Corinthians 13 test—the "Spiritual Love Meter." Every time I do this, I am so challenged because I realize how far I have to go in being close to him. As you read these verses, consider whether you have done these things in your relationship with God:

> **Love is patient, love is kind. It does not envy, it does not boast, it is not proud. It is not rude, it is not self-seeking, it is not easily angered, it keeps no record of wrongs. Love does not delight in evil but rejoices with the truth. It always protects, always trusts, always hopes, always perseveres.**
> **Love never fails. (1 Corinthians 13:4-8a)**

- *Love is patient:* How patient are you with God? If he does not answer your prayers right away, do you get mad and stop trusting him?

- *Love is kind:* When was the last time you did something kind for God, something that you didn't have to do, but that you knew would make him happy?

- *It does not envy:* Are you satisfied in life through your relationship with God, or do you envy your friends who are not Christians? Do you look at their lives and wish you didn't have to work so hard to be righteous?

- *It does not boast, it is not proud:* Are you prideful toward God—or toward the people he has put in your life? Do you resent or rebel against any of his commands?

- *It is not rude:* We sometimes do things to God that we would never do to other people. Do you let your time with him get interrupted and never bother to apologize? Do you *ever* apologize for things you have done that hurt him? Do you treat him with the respect and reverence he deserves?

- *It is not self-seeking:* Are you selfish in your relationship with him? Do you pray about anything besides yourself, your sin and the things you need, want and feel? Or do you ever take time just to thank God for who he is and all he has done in your life?

- *It always protects:* Do you defend God when his name is slandered? When people say things about him that are offensive or untrue, do you stand up for him? Think about how you would respond if you heard people gossiping about your boyfriend—you'd probably want to deck them on the spot!

- *Always trusts, always hopes:* How much do you trust God? Do you realize how much it hurts him when we do not trust him? When we doubt him or his promises, we are basically calling him a liar: We are saying that we do not think he will actually do the things he has promised.

• *Always perseveres:* What do you do when life gets challenging—when your faith is shaken, when God's commands are difficult to follow or when you don't understand why he is allowing you to suffer? Do you buckle under the pressure, or do you hang on to his word and to prayer, remaining strong and faithful in spite of your circumstances?

Pretty challenging test, huh? I encourage you to spend some time really thinking about each aspect of the Spiritual Love Meter. Decide to make some changes. Start simple and just pick two or three practical things you can do differently. Decide to become the best daughter, girl-friend and friend to God that you can possibly be.

But be forewarned: It can be easy to get overwhelmed when we realize how much we are lacking in our relationship with God. Teens seem especially prone to this feeling, and as a result, they never feel that they are close enough to him or are measuring up to his expectations. Such constant discouragement is neither healthy nor necessary, and it is not at all what God wants.

For many years of my Christian life, I never felt like I was close enough to God. Every time I heard a lesson about building a relationship with him, I felt terribly guilty and ended up in tears on many occasions. While I am certain that I did need to change some things, I also had a warped view of what it meant to be close to him. I kept searching for some gigantic warm-fuzzy, on-the-verge-of-tears-because-I'm-so-sorry-for-my-sins-and-so-grateful-for-the-cross feeling to fill me every time I prayed. I thought I was supposed to jump out of bed every morning grinning from ear to ear because I was so excited about reading my Bible and praying, and that I should spend a really long time doing so every day.

No wonder I felt so discouraged! No one in the world could live up to that standard in *any* relationship—with God or with another human being. For example, my parents are very much in love, but they don't wake up every morning with tears streaming down their faces and joy swelling their hearts as they declare, "I am so-o-o-o happy I am married to you, my sweet, wonderful, angelic sugar lump of love, and I want to spend every second of my existence having deep talks with you!" How utterly ridiculous! Now, they have definitely shared many special moments together during which they have expressed their love and even shed tears of appreciation for each other, and those times are very important. However, their marriage is not based solely on such moments. They love each other even when one of them has a bad day.

In the same way, we cannot have unrealistic expectations for our relationship with God. We simply need to make every effort to spend time with him daily and to grow closer to him consistently. There may be days when you don't feel like spending time with him—so what? It does not mean that you don't love God or that you never became a Christian. Those are the days when you deny yourself and take up your cross (Luke 9:23) and do what you know is right in spite of your feelings. Your emotions will catch up later. On some days your emotions may never get there—you may not get much out of your Bible reading, or you may not feel connected to God during some prayers. Every Christian has off days like this, but it does not automatically mean that they are hard-hearted wretches on the verge of falling away. If you experience these feelings on a continual basis, then talk about them and get some help from spiritual people.

It may be that you need to try some new things to keep you excited about your time with God.

Practically Speaking

There is no perfect formula to follow when spending time with God (otherwise known as "having a quiet time"), but certain things have proven especially effective. I always encourage people to set aside time to read and pray first thing every morning. The most convincing reason is because Jesus did it this way (Mark 1:35). Another is that it helps to prepare us spiritually for the day ahead. Satan throws numerous temptations and challenges at us throughout the day, and it is wise to prepare ourselves for battle beforehand. A soldier would never run out into battle wearing only his underwear; in the same way, we must clothe and arm ourselves with spiritual armor each morning (Ephesians 6:11-18).

School began for me at 7:30 am for most of my high school years, and it was always a challenge for me to get up early enough to have a decent quiet time. There were too many days when I ended up rushing around and barely had enough time to even open my Bible—and I could always tell a difference throughout the day. I had to become much more disciplined about going to bed early on weeknights so that I could get up on time. I also learned to have my quiet time first, before even leaving my room, so that even if I ended up rushing, my quiet time did not get cut out. Doing little things like preparing my clothes and book bag the night before helped me to move more quickly in the mornings. I also realized that it was unrealistic for me to spend tons of time with God on weekday mornings. I tried to use the weekends as days when I could set aside a longer period of time (preferably an hour) for being with God.

My goal was always to spend about thirty minutes with God in the mornings—fifteen minutes reading my Bible, and fifteen minutes praying. On the days when I was unable to spend a long time with God, or when I missed my quiet time altogether, I had to learn to be close to God throughout the day anyway. I often felt guilty all day and felt that God was not with me, but I had to realize that God was with me no matter what had happened that morning. My mom taught me to rely on what she calls "bullet prayers," quick prayers to God throughout the day. Sometimes I would step into a bathroom stall between classes and ask him for quick help, or take a few minutes during lunch to pray. I was far from perfect in any of these areas—in fact, having consistent quiet times was a real struggle for me. I had to work on it every day, get people to help me change, and trust that God would be patient with me as I fought to make progress.

Another important thing for teens to grasp is that quiet times should not be guilt sessions. I used to think that I had to focus on my sins and repentance during every quiet time, that my prayers were supposed to revolve around me dredging up every single sin or temptation I could remember, conjuring up feelings of guilt as I confessed them to God. I thought I couldn't talk to God or move on until I had dealt with every sin in my heart. No wonder I sometimes dreaded my quiet times and procrastinated as long as possible before having them! I didn't understand that a quiet time was the time that I could use to become closer to God, just as I spent time with my family and friends. I didn't expect myself to be perfect in those relationships, yet somehow I expected perfection from myself in my times with God.

I must have frustrated him continually during those days. He just wanted to talk to me and get close to me by hearing about my thoughts, needs, dreams and desires, but I insisted on a sin-focused relationship. If you are enslaved to guilt and the desire for perfection, I encourage you to study the book of Galatians. Look at the way God feels about people who insist on legalism and perfection as opposed to those who live by grace and the Spirit. And chill out! Stop making God out to be an ogre and just be his child!

Keeping It Fresh

One of the biggest challenges in building a relationship with God is in keeping it exciting day after day. The key for all disciples, and teens in particular, since they are not exactly known for the length of their attention spans—is keeping variety in your quiet times. Don't let yourself get into a rut in which you always do the same thing day after day—spice things up so you don't get bored! One especially helpful idea is to go outside. I love sitting on our back porch to read and pray, where I can admire the beauty of all God has made. Somehow I feel so much closer to him. Here are some other things that have helped me:

Prayer

- *Take prayer walks*. Again, this takes you out of your house and into God's creation.

- *Write down your prayers sometimes*. This always helps me when I'm having trouble concentrating as I pray. Your prayer will move a little slower, but your mind won't wander as much.

- *Have "thankful prayers."* Whenever I found myself being negative or ungrateful, I made myself have prayers in which I only thanked or praised God. It sounds easy, but it's quite a challenge. However, I guarantee you will be much happier by the time you get off your knees.

- *Pray through the Lord's prayer*. Read Luke 11:1-4. Use it as a pattern for your prayers. This will keep you from becoming selfish, monotonous or guilty in your prayers because you praise God, pray for his kingdom and surrender to his will in your life and in your family's life—all before you pray about your own needs and sins.

- *Pray through a psalm.*

Bible Study

- *Study out some of the teens or young adults in the Bible*—there are more of them than you would guess! Study people like Esther, Ruth, Mary, David, Jonathan, Timothy, John Mark, Jeremiah, Joseph (in the Old Testament), Rebekah, Isaac and Daniel (and the list goes on).

- *The Proverbs are an excellent practical study for teens.* They deal with every area of life, from friendships, to work, to money.

- *Study Psalm 119.* It's long, and it will take you a while, but it is addressed to young people.

- *Use a concordance to help you study topics that interest you.*

- *Study a particular book of the Bible.*

- *Read other spiritual books besides the Bible.* DPI publishes books written by fellow disciples, and there are countless other books written by spiritual people that can serve as a tremendous asset to your study times.

- *Ask some of your Christian friends what they are reading or for suggestions.* Write up quiet times for each other!

You have the unusual privilege of beginning to build a relationship with God at a young age. You join the ranks of so many great Biblical leaders who began to seek God and develop a heart for him as children and as teens.

One of my favorite characters of all time is David, who developed a relationship with God on his own while shepherding his father's flocks. No one made him do it, but of his own accord he spent the lonely hours praying, meditating, singing and writing psalms to God. Some of the psalms he wrote as a teenager are among the most stirring parts of the entire Bible. David's heart for God as a young man led him to be called "a man after God's own heart," and set him apart as the greatest king Israel ever had.

You don't have to wait until you are older or more mature to seek God—seek his face now! If he begins molding your character now, he alone knows what he can do with you by the time you hit college, much less your adult years!

A relationship with God is the solution to every challenge you will face over the next few years, whether you simply struggle with insecurity, or deal with a move, or face difficulties in your family life. God will be the strength, security and confidence you need to make it through the next few years. He's waiting with bated breath for you to simply reach out to him. All it takes is for you to open your mouth and say, "Father."

3. Dating

"I have come that they may have life,
and have it to the full."
JOHN 10:10

As a little girl, I remember asking my mom, "Who am I going to marry?" She would always reply, "Somewhere there's a little boy, and God is working on him right now to get him ready for you." My eyes would widen as an image of a faceless little boy flitted across my mind. Then Mom and I would pray for God to prepare him to be my husband one day and help him grow up to love his Father in Heaven.

As I grew old enough to understand more of what it meant to be in love, and as I developed those infamous instigators of "love"—hormones—I became a total sap. I adored romantic movies, and I prayed often that God would give me a romance as exciting and passionate as those I saw on the big screen.

I went on my first date when I was in the eighth grade—and absolutely hated it! My extreme nervousness made the entire evening torturous, and I couldn't wait to go home. At the end of the night, I wept as I told my parents, "I never want to go on another date again! I hate dates!" Thankfully, my resolve didn't last too long. I did go on other dates, and they got much better. By my sophomore year in high school, going on dates wasn't enough—I dreamed of finding "the one" for me and falling madly in love.

Although I had one special relationship that lasted for about a year in high school, God did not bless me with my dream relationship for a long time—not until I learned to truly trust his perfect plan for my life and future marriage. It is so important for teen women to develop this level of trust in God's plans. During our teen years we can tend to think of falling in love as the be-all and the end-all of existence. Too many of us try to rush into dating relationships instead of waiting for God to bless us with the man he has hand-chosen for us. God does not give us dating relationships until he feels we are spiritually and emotionally ready for them. For many of us, this means learning to trust him patiently.

I love the story of Isaac and Rebekah in Genesis 24, and I encourage you to read it as well. It describes the way God found a wife for Isaac. God's plans are so detailed and are exactly tailored to meet our needs. Do you believe that even now God is working to one day give you an incredible marriage beyond what you can imagine? When we honestly trust this, it makes it much easier to patiently wait for God to unfold his plan at the time he knows will be best for us.

Christian Dating

Meanwhile, as we wait for God to one day bless us with an incredible marriage, how should we view dating in general? Many of us have an unspiritual view of dating, and unless we learn to view it in a godly way, we are setting ourselves up for a fall. The purpose of dating is to build great friendships. If you would start to view dating in this way, you would be amazed at the amount of pressure it would take off you.

Many of us put enormous expectations on dates. We spend the entire time analyzing whether or not we feel all ooey-gooey in love with this person and want to have children with them one day. We are seeking a "romantic experience" rather than a normal friendship, and as a result, we never really get to know them. Even if we do continue to go on other dates with that person, we base the so-called relationship on mere infatuation, rather than on true friendship and spiritual qualities.

Drill it into your head that going on a date with someone doesn't mean you must know immediately whether or not you like them and want to marry them. I know very few people who end up with the person they think they are in love with in high school—even though they may swear at the time that they want to spend the rest of their lives with them.

Others of us are not worried about who we are going to fall in love with or marry—no, we think members of the opposite sex are aliens (or some strange, mysterious species). We are scared to death to be around them. We are totally cool hanging out with our friends, laughing and talking our heads off, but as soon as one of the intimidating "others" comes around, we get so nervous that we act like idiots. We either start laughing and talking nonstop, or we go hide in a corner and do our best impression of a rock. Spending time with the opposite sex just hanging out or going on dates (if we feel able to handle it without self-destructing) is important for those of us who feel this way: It teaches us to be friends with them in the same way (well, in almost the same way!) as we are friends with members of our own sex.

Another main reason for dating is simply to have fun! It is not designed to be miserable and awkward, although some of us have allowed it to make us feel this way. Again, if we could learn to view the opposite sex as friends, we would have more fun and be relaxed when hanging out with them. When you are around them, don't allow yourself to have different expectations than you would for spending time with other friends. I know this is what I did when I first started developing friendships and dating consistently. I put all sorts of expectations on myself and on my date instead of just enjoying hanging out together.

Who to Date

Although you are dating to build friendships, not to find a future spouse, it is still important that you choose wisely those whom you date. I was always very careful to only go out with guys I knew who were trustworthy, responsible and most importantly, strong disciples.

The Bible does not specifically address dating, but wise guidelines can be developed from Biblical principles. There is no command that says disciples should only date other disciples, although 2 Corinthians 6:14-17 lays down a principle which I believe applies to dating relationships. It reads:

> **Do not be yoked together with unbelievers. For what do righteousness and wickedness have in common? Or what fellowship can light have with darkness? What harmony is there between Christ and Belial? What does a believer have in common with an unbeliever? What agreement is there between the temple of God and idols? For we are the temple of the living God. As God has said: "I will live with them and walk among them, and I will be their God, and they will be my people."**

> **"Therefore come out from them**
> **and be separate,**
> **says the Lord.**
> **Touch no unclean thing,**
> **and I will receive you."**
> **(2 Corinthians 6:14-17)**

I have always had a number of friends at church and at school, but my Christian friends have always been my closest relationships. We simply have more in common because we share deep Biblical convictions, a love for God that is foremost in our lives, and the same purpose of spreading the good news wherever we can. My best friends have always been people who continually call me higher spiritually and those with whom I can share my feelings and struggles.

Since the purpose of dating is to develop close friendships, it only seems natural that we would want to date those with whom we share the most important convictions. I have always wanted to date guys who helped bring me closer to God, period. My emotions were quite fickle in high school, particularly when it came to affairs of the heart, and so I determined never to put myself in a situation that might lead me to have feelings for a guy who did not love God as I did. It's not that I didn't notice or even find myself attracted in some ways to guys who were not Christians. I would have been blind not to notice that some of them were good-looking or had great personalities! But I knew that were I to go out with those guys and allow myself the possibility of liking them, my relationship with God would suffer. There were several times that I had to hold my emotions in tight rein, and times when I had to distance myself a bit from certain guys with whom I was tempted to flirt.

Sadly, also, I knew that sexual sin was running rampant around me. Many of my friends have tremendous regret and emotional scars because they began to compromise sexually in middle school or in high school. I never wanted to go out with a guy unless I was absolutely certain that he shared my convictions about purity. Going on a date was scary enough without having to worry about whether or not the guy was going to do anything inappropriate! The only way I knew to do this was to date young men who I knew were strong Christians.

I have never regretted this decision. In no way did it hinder me from going out as many times as my friends at school did. If anything, I went out much more often than they did. They always wondered where I met cool guys who treated me with such respect. I never had to worry about a thing except what to wear, how to avoid spilling food all over myself and remembering to let him open the doors for me!

So, what do you do when a guy asks you out, and he's not a Christian? I always tried to be honest instead of just giving some scheduling excuse for why I couldn't go. My response was usually something like this: "Thanks so much for asking me, but I only go out with people I know really well, which ends up being the guys who go to church with me." I often added, "I go to a really great church, and you're welcome to visit with me sometime, if you want to!" That was it—I didn't go into some long theological explanation, and I didn't apologize. I was very nice and polite, and always thanked them for the invitation, but I made it clear where I stood. No one ever gave me a hard time about that—in fact they usually respected me for it, even though they might not have completely understood. Actually, several guys who asked me out in high school did visit the church with me. I'm not sure that their motivations were entirely spiritual, but at least they had the opportunity to hear the Bible preached!

I sometimes felt tremendously guilty if I ever found myself noticing a guy at school and feeling attracted to him. I remember several times when I tearfully confessed such feelings to my mom. She always responded in the same way: She encouraged me to care enough about them to share my faith with them and to pray that one day they could become Christians. If they did, who knew what might happen then? My feelings were not sinful—I just had to decide not to allow them to progress any further and not to act on them in any way.

How to Date

When we do get asked out by a guy, what do we do? What should a date be like? My first few dates were actually to church functions. My parents drove me, and I met my date there. We then were free to hang out with all our friends at church together, which made things a little less scary. I always encourage people, especially teens, to go out on dates with at least one other couple.

If you haven't been on dates before, I would encourage you to get some help on dating etiquette before you go on your first date. I really wish I had done that, because I was absolutely clueless about how things should go on my first few dates.

As I mentioned earlier, my first date was an absolute disaster. David and I went to a church party. We were supposed to be on a double date with two other teens in the church, but the other guy never showed up, and my friend Jessica abandoned us in her distress. As a result, my date and I were stuck hanging out together all night, with very little to talk about and no one else to help the conversation along. I was so nervous that I could barely think up a single thing to say the whole night. I didn't realize that guys usually do the paying on dates, so when he kept offering to buy me a dessert, I was afraid to let him buy me anything. (How I managed to be so clueless, I do not know!) Plus, I had always had a fear of dancing, so when the band started playing, you can imagine my dismay. Thankfully, people just stood in the audience and sang along that night!

My first "car date"—when my date Sergio picked me up at my house in his car—was equally humiliating, although I was not quite as miserable. We went out once again with my friend Jessica, whose date actually showed up this time. We planned to attend a wedding at church together and to go out to dinner afterward. I had no idea that Sergio would want to open my car door and let me sit in the front seat with him. I just assumed that since I was the smallest one, I would sit in the back seat with Jessica. There was a tremendously awkward moment as I stood by the back door yapping away with Jessica, waiting for the guys to get in and unlock the back door. Everyone stood around waiting for me to get a clue for a few moments, until Jessica finally elbowed me and hissed, "Elizabeth, Sergio wants to open the door for you. You're supposed to sit up front."

Then, when we arrived at the wedding, I opened my door and got out without a thought. Sergio objected and insisted that I let him open the door and let me out. I don't know what got into me the rest of the night, but I proceeded to walk into a pole, lock my car door so that Sergio couldn't let me out, forget several more times to wait for him to open my door, and discovered a hair in my taco salad at Taco Bell. (Yes, this was an extremely high-class date!)

The evening ended in a fittingly glorious manner. As we pulled into my driveway, I finally managed to remember to wait for Sergio to open my door, and I even unlocked the door for him. My victory was soon lost, however. As he opened the door of my house to let me in, I started to walk in and realized too late that my dad had left his tuxedo lying in the doorway so he would not forget to return it the next day. I almost stepped on the tuxedo, but managed to straddle it at the last moment, leaving my left foot still on the doorstep, half out of my shoe. Sergio shut the door, catching my shoe in it. As I stood there trying to maintain my balance, he opened the door once more, looked down and said profoundly, "Your shoe." Without waiting for me to reply, he shut the door once more, leaving me still straddled across the tuxedo. As I recounted the night's misadventures to my parents later on, we found ourselves in fits of laughter. I was still unsure of whether I ever wanted to venture out on another date again.

Unfortunately, these two stories are not my only nightmare date stories. Were I to tell them all, it might take up several chapters! I do not have time to tell about when I choked on a piece of candy while riding home from a date and had to pull over to throw up on the side of the highway, or about the time I thought I was on a date but wasn't. My only consolation is that maybe my mishaps can help others avoid the same humiliation I have experienced! Here are some of the things I have learned:

- *Always double-date.* Trust me on this one. It is always more fun when you are with a larger group, especially when you do not know your date particularly well. I don't know about you, but I have a hard time sustaining an interesting conversation with the same person for two or three hours, especially if I am just getting to know the person. Dates have the potential to be tremendously awkward experiences, and it always helps to have other people around to help keep the conversation going. Also, when you go out with a group of people, not only do you get to know your date, but you also have the opportunity to become closer to several other people throughout the evening. Double-dating also protects you from any sexual temptations Satan might throw your way. It's hard to get too snuggly with someone you like when other Christians are around!

- *Consider postponing dating until you are in high school.* I realize that some of you may still be in middle school (still called junior high in some places), and it is my feeling that middle-school age is too young to go on dates. Obviously, this is not a rule found anywhere in the Bible, and some people would probably disagree with it. But I can only tell you what I think based on my personal experience and observation.

    I went on a few dates when I was still in the eighth grade, and as you have already heard, they were absolutely humiliating disasters! I wish I had avoided dating altogether until I was a bit more mature and confident. By doing so I could have spared myself a great deal of unnecessary embarrassment and heartache. I think I was just a little too young to be able to handle dating at fourteen. By the time I was a freshman, however, I had grown in my confidence and social skills so that I felt much more comfortable and began to enjoy dating. I suggest that you talk this over with your parents to come to a decision.

- *If you are not familiar with dating etiquette, ask someone to help you before you go on your first few dates.* There was a lot about dating that I should have known, but didn't—simple things like letting my date open the car door for me and riding next to him in the car.

- *Carry money with you, just in case.* Guys do the paying most of the time, but it never hurts to be prepared.

- *If you don't know your date very well, try to find out about his interests.* I thought beforehand about topics we could discuss, just in case the conversation lagged a bit. If I knew what he liked, it helped me to think of questions I could ask him to get a discussion going again.

- *Have balanced conversation.* It is important that you get to know your date on a spiritual level instead of talking only about superficial things. But don't go overboard and try to be the next apostle, insisting on having intense spiritual discussions the entire time.

- *Don't talk the whole time!* This sounds silly for me to even say, but I have done this before. I also have witnessed many other teenage girls doing the same thing. Sometimes when we get nervous, we try to cover it up by talking nonstop. Others of us are just so selfish that we love to talk about ourselves all the time. There is nothing more obnoxious than a girl or woman who can't stop prattling.

- *On the flip side, don't sit there mute, either.* Don't be so nervous or shy that you force your date to work really hard in order to draw you into a conversation.

- *Avoid conversations about love interests.* Whether you "like" your date or not, it is inappropriate to probe into one another's love life. Don't go confessing that you think he or she is the most attractive person you've ever laid eyes on, and by all means, don't ask them what they think about you!

The Next Step

So, what if you do find yourself interested in a particular brother or sister? If you are attracted to a disciple, consider how strong they are spiritually before you decide whether or not you are "in love" with them. I never wanted to give my heart to someone who was not going to challenge me spiritually and help me become closer and more committed to God. A relationship based merely on outward appearance might be fun for a little while, but such relationships usually end up distracting us from God rather than drawing us nearer to him.

If they are indeed spiritual, then there is nothing wrong with forming a special friendship with them. However, it is important that you not decide to do this on your own. Get a lot of advice from spiritual people who can guide you—particularly from the person discipling you, from your teen leader and from your parents (especially if they are disciples). They can help you determine how often you should talk on the phone and go out with them.

I had one such relationship during my sophomore and junior years in high school. We lived a ways away from each other and so did not see one another very often. During the week we talked on the phone twice a week, but not for hours on end, mind you, and sent each other one letter. We went on one date a month, always with other friends. We had so much fun and did not feel burdened by these parameters.

Although we cared a lot about each other at the time, our parents never wanted us to date steady. I did not fully understand their reasoning at the time—I really wanted to have an official boyfriend I could hold hands with! But looking back now, I am extremely thankful for my parents' wisdom. They were simply protecting me from heartache. They understood that our feelings as teenagers were fickle and that even though we firmly declared our love for each other at the time, we might change our minds later! They knew that we had dated very few people and did not really know who all was out there to date. What would happen if we committed ourselves to a relationship, and one of us met someone else whom we might want to get to know better? We would be torn and forced to decide whether to completely break off the dating relationship, or to simply ignore our other interest. Hence, it was much better for us to have a relationship less serious than an official dating relationship. We knew that we had feelings for each other and enjoyed special talks and dates, but we were not officially bound only to each other. Later on, when my family moved away and our feelings for each other began to cool, there was no emotional break-up to shatter our hearts or our friendship.

My younger brother David has had a similar relationship for the past few years. They know that they care deeply for each other and have gone on a number of special dates. They even went to prom together. However, they have left one another with the freedom to date others, and this freedom has served them well, particularly since they do not live in the same place. Once they are both in college, a bit more mature and have dated other people, they can decide whether or not they are still interested in each other.

As a result of these personal experiences, I firmly believe that most high-school students should not officially date one person. Again, this is a personal conviction and by no means a rule. I have had several Christian friends who steady dated in high school, and they might tell you differently. However, every one of those people has since broken up with their high school boyfriends and girlfriends and thus experienced emotional trauma that my brother and I have been able to avoid. If you do share a mutual interest, it is up to you to get help from godly people who will help you to decide what direction you should take in that relationship.

Absolute Purity

> But among you there must not be even a hint of sexual immorality, or of any kind of impurity, or of greed, because these are improper for God's holy people. (Ephesians 5:3)

> The body is not meant for sexual immorality, but for the Lord, and the Lord for the body. (1 Corinthians 6:13b)

> Flee from sexual immorality. All other sins a man commits are outside his body, but he who sins sexually sins against his own body. Do you not know that your body is a temple of the Holy Spirit, who is in you, whom you have received from God? You are not your own; you were bought at a price. Therefore honor God with your body. (1 Corinthians 6:18-20)

There is never a question about how God feels about sexual immorality and impurity: They are absolutely wrong and are not even an option for those who claim to love him. There should be nothing in our lives that even remotely suggests any immorality or impurity ("not even a hint"). What exactly does it mean to be sexually immoral or impure? Immorality refers to any sex outside of marriage, including premarital sex, an adulterous relationship while married, homosexual sex and bestiality (sex with animals). Impurity includes all the things that are sexual in nature and that can lead up to sex—things like lust, masturbation, French kissing, petting and oral sex.

It is not that sex itself is bad or dirty. God made it, and he made it to feel good on purpose. The book of Song of Solomon celebrates the joy of marital romance and sexual relations. God created sex to be a special experience reserved only for a husband and wife. Having sex is an intimate experience that somehow knits souls together in a way that nothing else does. The two become one flesh, as it says in Genesis 2:24. God wants each of us to one day experience a fulfilling and exciting sexual life within the bounds of a loving, close marriage. Once we have sex with a person, we give them a part of ourselves—a part that we can never take back.

God prohibits sex not to punish us, but to help us and protect us. He is helping us to have the best marriages we can possibly have one day, and he wants to protect us from physical and emotional harm. Not only are there physical risks in having sex—risks like acquiring painful sexually transmitted diseases and the HIV virus, or becoming pregnant—but the emotional consequences can be devastating and leave lifelong scars. Many of my friends had sex with guys who they thought they were in love with and who they planned to marry at the time. But the relationships never lasted, and my friends were left with the painful knowledge that they had given a part of their very souls to men they might never speak to or see again. God's desire is to spare us this kind of pain—he is only looking out for our best interests.

The teenage years are the time in life when many people first become sexually aware. Our hormones stir up all sorts of strange new feelings, physically and emotionally. We find ourselves noticing the opposite sex, and suddenly they no longer seem like the annoying pests they were in elementary and middle school. Our bodies develop, and we begin to look and feel like adults.

It is up to us to decide what to do with the changes and the awareness. Unfortunately, sexual sin is rampant among most teenagers. Most of the people I know first began to compromise sexually while in middle school and especially in high school. It may have started with a little kiss while hiding off in a corner somewhere, but then progressed to French kissing and petting. Some held off for a while, but many ended up losing their virginity while still high school students. I have studied the Bible with countless women, and I am now surprised when one tells me that she has never had sex.

The best way I know to avoid falling into impurity or immorality is to begin with your mind. Most sexual sin begins in the form of lust, or thinking sexual thoughts about people. Jesus says in Matthew 5:28 that lustful thoughts are every bit as serious as actual sexual involvement: "But I tell you that anyone who looks at a woman lustfully has already committed adultery with her in his heart." It is not okay for us to allow our thoughts to get carried away. We must "take captive every thought to make it obedient to Christ" (2 Corinthians 10:5).

I was so afraid as a teen of being lustful that I would get really paranoid about it. There were times when I felt like I couldn't even look at a guy because I was so afraid that I might look at him in a sexual way. Paranoia about lust seems to be a fairly common phenomenon among teenage disciples, but it is not a healthy way for us to live. Part of our problem is that many of us have only vague ideas about what lust is, and so we feel guilty for having thoughts that aren't even sinful. Perhaps these guidelines will help you:

Lust Is Not

• *Lust is not noticing that someone is attractive.* There is absolutely nothing wrong with this! I would be concerned about you if you never found anyone attractive.

• *Lust is not noticing that someone is attractive and having an involuntary bodily reaction.* Sometimes our bodies respond of their own accord, before we know what's happening. Some people have more sensitive bodies than others, but just experiencing a sexual feeling does not necessarily mean that you are being lustful.

• *Lust is not accidentally looking at sexual areas of the body.* Sometimes our eyes stray, and we look at things we don't really intend to stare at. I felt so nervous about this that I felt like I had to look straight ahead, never down, so I wouldn't accidentally see a body part that I shouldn't be looking at.

• *Lust is not having a sexual thought cross your mind.* I felt guilty any time I had any sort of sexual thought, but did not realize that such thoughts were merely temptations. Our culture is so sex saturated that Satan has plenty of ammunition to use against us. We are not in control of every weird thought that Satan throws into our heads—we are only responsible for what we do with those thoughts once we have them. Just think of such thoughts as arrows Satan is shooting through your mind. Your job is to deflect these arrows by quickly taking the thought captive and thinking about something else instead.

Lust Is

• *Lust is allowing yourself to imagine sexual experiences in your head—* what it would feel like to touch each other or to sleep together. Indulging in fantasies.

• *Lust is scanning another person's body with your eyes, deliberately looking at their physique*—particularly in sexual areas of the body—and undressing them in your mind.

It's really that simple. For those of you who struggle with sexual thoughts or with paranoia about lust, the best thing to do is to fill your mind with other, more pure thoughts. Instead of fighting a defensive battle in which you are always trying to fight off evil thoughts, fill your head with so many good thoughts that you don't have any room left over. Romans 12:21 teaches, "Do not be overcome by evil, but overcome evil with good." Overcome bad thoughts by filling your mind with good ones.

My dad offered me a profound piece of advice when I was struggling with these things. He told me that I could only think about one thing at a time, so I should just decide that I would always think about one good, pure thing! One way to do this is by praying. When you feel Satan preparing to throw temptations your way, stop and pray for other people, or thank God for your blessings. Another way of doing this—and it sounds silly, but it works—is just to sing a song in your head. I used to sing "Jesus Loves Me" over and over in my mind or under my breath whenever I was fighting off weird or sinful thoughts. Another option is to just think about positive things. Philippians 4:8 teaches us what we should meditate upon:

Finally, brothers, whatever is true, whatever is noble, whatever is right, whatever is pure, whatever is lovely, whatever is admirable—if anything is excellent or praiseworthy—think about such things. (Philippians 4:8)

Write down a list of the things you can think about that fit these descriptions. You could even carry around a Bible verse like this one on an index card to read whenever you feel thoughts may be coming your way. The most important thing to remember is to have deep convictions about not being lustful, but avoiding paranoia. Paranoia just makes it so much worse. You end up thinking, "Don't lust, don't lust, don't lust," over and over in your head, so of course because you're thinking about *not* lusting, you're going to have sexual thoughts all over the place!

Dealing with Mistakes

Many teenagers have already been involved in sexual sin by the time they become Christians, and sadly, some even succumb to temptation as disciples. If you are one of those people, but have never been open about it, it is imperative that you talk to a mature disciple you can trust—and that you talk about it *now*. Proverbs 28:13 says, "He who conceals his sins does not prosper, but whoever confesses and renounces them finds mercy." You will always be a slave to guilt, shame and deceit until you confess what you are holding in your heart.

Mature Christians will not condemn you as the worst person alive, they will not kick you out of the church and they will not run around telling everyone else what you have done. They will, however, deal with your sin in a forthright way. They will continue to challenge you until you have truly repented in the manner that God expects, but this is not something to be afraid of. It may not be the most pleasant or fun time of your life, but it will ultimately be the most refreshing. Do not allow pride and fear to keep you separated from God or his people any longer. Let God bring you back into a close relationship with him.

Others of you may have already confessed and repented of sexual sin, but remain slaves to guilt. You must realize that if you are a disciple, your sins—all of them—have been completely forgiven and forgotten by God. Satan may be trying to torment you with guilt and shame, but do not allow him the victory he seeks. Study out the grace and forgiveness of God, and know that in his eyes, you are now as pure as you were on the day of your birth. You can live your life and go on dates with a clear conscience and a peaceful heart.

The more I have seen of dating in the world, the more thankful I become for dating in the kingdom. We are so blessed! My friends in the world have always been jealous of my dating life, even during the years when I was not dating a particular person, and even more so now that I have such an incredible boyfriend. As disciples, we are treated like royalty! Ask your friends in the world when they last went on a date, how they were asked and what the date was like. You'll know what I mean. Dating in God's kingdom is a privilege and will provide you with some of the most fun, memorable experiences of your life.

I mentioned that I used to sit, misty-eyed, in sappy movies and pray that God would give me a romance as exciting and passionate as what I saw on the screen. During my junior year of high school I met a guy who was in town visiting his brother at a college near my home. He came to visit my church with his parents, who had known my parents many years ago when we lived in Florida. He was not a Christian, but there was something about him that I liked right away (maybe it was the fact that he was a really good-looking football player!). Over the next year or so, our families spent time together on several occasions, and I found myself enjoying getting to know him. The next fall he decided to attend Duke University, which is only twenty minutes away from my home—and I was just a little bit excited.

One night our family had a devotional together, and each of us wrote down a list of things we planned to pray about every day. I listed seven things, one of which was that he would become a Christian when he moved here. I prayed for him every day for months, especially once I also decided to attend Duke! Sure enough, when he moved to North Carolina, he started studying the Bible with some of the guys at church as soon as he arrived. Shortly thereafter, he became a Christian. The two of us quickly became best friends as we worked together to build a campus ministry at Duke. Now, two-and-a-half years later, we are dating steady and are very much in love!

God has blessed me with the kind of relationship I have always dreamed about having, and I would not trade it for anything. I am so thankful that Kevin and I decided to build our relationship in the way God intended and that neither of us pursued anything more than a friendship before he became a Christian. Now Kevin has grown so much spiritually that, even though I am an older Christian than he is, he continually calls me higher in my walk with God. We share the same goals and dreams in life—to win as many as possible to Christ while we are here at Duke, and one day to work in the ministry together elsewhere.

I had to wait for what seemed like a million years, but God has truly blessed me. Romance in the kingdom is indescribably wonderful, and I believe that God holds it in store for every one of his faithful children. If you will only wait patiently and keep a spiritual focus, at the proper time he will bring your Prince Charming into your life to sweep you off your feet and carry you into the sunset—or he'll bring you the girl of your dreams. It may not be when you are seventeen—although in my case, it was, but I didn't know it for several years. Who knows when it will happen to you? The agony of waiting is, in some twisted way, a part of the "fun" of falling in love. It may not seem fun now, but several years from now you may look back at this time with a smile and a knowing shake of your head—and just burst out laughing...you just wait!

4. Friendships

"A new command I give you: Love one another.
As I have loved you, so you must love
one another. By this all men will know that
you are my disciples, if you love one another."
JOHN 13:34-35

*No one knows the real me. If they knew what I am really like, they'd
never want to talk to me again. No one cares about me. Everyone else has
best friends except me. I'm just not meant to have close friends.*

Do these thoughts sound a little familiar? I thought and felt every
one of these things at different times during my teen years—and sometimes I felt all of them at once! There is something about friendship and
adolescence that doesn't naturally fit together well. Most teens I know
have a difficult time forming close relationships, even by the world's standard of closeness. Once you include spirituality as a requirement for closeness, most teens fail miserably. Teens are notorious for doing anything
and compromising everything in order to be liked and to gain friends—but
even so, most remain lonely.

I'm not just talking about people who are not disciples. I believe that
Satan loves to torment teenage Christians with their shortcomings in building friendships. Many disciples have no clue how to be close to people,
especially in a spiritual sense. They do not understand how to be vulnerable with others and to talk on a deep level. Perhaps they are insecure,
constantly worried about what people would think if they knew their weaknesses and sins; maybe they pride themselves on their independence and

feel they do not need people in their lives; maybe they are unspiritual and shallow, and do not understand what it means to have a godly friendship; or perhaps they desperately want to be close to people, but have no idea where to begin.

Many teens enter the kingdom of God with great expectations of the deep friendships they are going to build as Christians but quickly fall victim to Satan's attacks. He lies to them, planting doubts, insecurities, fears and pride in their hearts and minds. Some find themselves continually haunted by thoughts like those mentioned at the beginning of this chapter.

I was one of those people. It was not easy for me to build friendships in high school. I spent my middle school years and the first part of high school feeling different and alone, even after becoming a Christian. I was insecure, proud and selfish at the same time—not a good recipe for getting to know people. I felt that my sins were unique and much worse than everyone else's and was afraid to let others know the real me. I had strange ideas about what it meant to be close to people. I thought that unless I told them every single detail about myself, including every sin, weakness and weird thought I ever had, we could not be close. I was searching for someone with whom I had everything in common, the perfect friend.

It was not until my family moved to New Jersey the summer before my sophomore year that I finally learned to have close friendships. I had begun to outgrow some of my insecurities, but I needed the opportunity to start over somewhere new, where people did not view me in the same way I had been for the previous few years. I decided during the long car ride up to New Jersey that I would no longer be the person I had been— that no one in my new home had to think of me as being a shy, insecure, quiet person.

I am amazed at God's timing, because within just a day or so of our move, I met the girl who was quickly to become the best friend I ever had. Everything just clicked right between Sara and me. Our personalities were different, but we understood each other in a way I had never before experienced. She was the epitome of a people person—everywhere she went, she made friends in a moment, and being close to her taught me how to get close to others as well. I also quickly hit it off with several of the other teens in the New York church, and found myself rapidly growing in confidence and happiness. I still experienced struggles throughout high school, and the friendships I formed were far from perfect, but at least I now had some victories to go on. I still had a great deal to learn, but I no longer felt like a complete failure at relationships. I had the confidence to battle through whatever relational challenges I faced.

After experiencing such great change in my own life, I am convinced that teens do not have to be weird, relationally challenged people who are simply unable to have friends. All that is required for most teens is that they mature out of some of their strange, worldly ways of thinking and learn what God says about how to build friendships.

How to Build Great Friendships

I wish I could give you a simple formula by which you can instantly attain great friendships—"Ten Easy Steps to Having a Best Friend"—but unfortunately, no such recipe exists. The best place to start is by identifying the obstacles you have erected in your heart that keep people at a distance and to bulldoze those obstacles with the help of the Bible and the Holy Spirit.

The biggest problem I have seen in myself and in teenagers in general is that we have distorted, unrealistic expectations of what a friend is. I did not understand what it meant to be open and vulnerable with people and to let them know the real Elizabeth with all her complicated feelings and thoughts. I equated spirituality in a relationship with intensity and confession of sin. I thought that a friend had to know every gory detail of my life and especially of my weaknesses and sins in order to truly be close to me. I also felt that we had to have everything in common in order to even begin to build a friendship.

Some of those ideas may sound pretty ridiculous to some of you, but for others, they may define your own thoughts about friendship. Let me just identify and dispel some common misconceptions about what should be expected in relationships:

- *Being open and honest about yourself does not mean confessing every hideous detail about your weaknesses and sins.* It is indeed very important that we are open with people about our true selves, because it helps us realize that we are not the only ones in the world who struggle with our particular sins, and it enables us to get help in changing. However, it is logistically impossible for every friend in our lives to know every detail about our sins. Sometimes it is sufficient for people just to know that we struggle with a certain sin, which is enough for them to understand and help us. If I were to confess to people my every sin, we would have to sit in a room for about twenty hours a day as I recounted my every thought. How utterly ridiculous! Yet so many of us feel distant from people unless we confess our every thought to them. Part of this feeling stems from a lack of understanding of God's grace, and part of it from our fear that if people knew how sinful we really are, they would run away from us, shrieking in horror. If we expect ourselves to confess every evil thought we have, it forces people to be our confession partners instead of our friends, and it puts a weird pressure on the relationship. This strange thinking seems particularly influential in our relationships with our disciplers. Disciplers are meant to be our friends who happen to be more mature than us spiritually and who help to guide us closer to God—not priests who continually rebuke us and who possess the power to absolve us of guilt once we confess.

- *You do not have to magically "click" with a person in order to become close friends.* Many of us keep waiting for the stars to align just right so that we meet the perfect friend, one who understands and sympathizes with every single thought and feeling we have ever had. We think we should be overtaken by warm fuzzies every time we speak to them. I have news for you: The perfect friend does not exist! There may be certain people with whom you experience a unique and special bond, but most of us will find only a small number of friends like this in our lifetime. Because Sara and I hit it off so quickly and so well, I expected that every close relationship should function in that same way. Therefore I did not subsequently give my heart to people unless I experienced that special spark in our relationship—and this kept me from being close to many people for years. Friendship is not a magical feeling. It is a decision to give your heart to a person in spite of any differences you may have.

- *You do not have to be exactly like another person to be "best friends."* It's wonderful when we discover people who share a lot in common with us. However we can and should also be close to people who are different from us. It is not necessary to love all the same music, wear the same clothes, play the same sports or share all the same views on life. We must learn to appreciate many kinds of people and to enjoy our differences.

- *You can have more than one "best friend," and your friendships should not all be ranked in order of closeness.* Teenagers, and teenage girls in particular, can be highly competitive and selfish in our friendships. We feel threatened if anyone else starts to befriend our "best friend," and in our own minds we have ranked each friend in order of their closeness to us. This is worldly thinking, completely unsuitable for disciples of Jesus.

   Will some friends be closer to us than others? Absolutely. When we become preoccupied with figuring out who is most important to us, we are bound to hurt people, and ultimately ourselves as well. We will end up with a very narrow circle of friends and will never experience the joy of making new friends, or of having a larger group of people we feel close to. Not only will we never get to know anyone new, but our selfishness, jealousy and insecurity will ultimately destroy the very relationships we are trying to protect.

   I struggled with every one of these things in high school, and they definitely made my life much more difficult, complicated and lonely than it needed to be. I urge you to figure out which misconceptions you hold and to fight to change the way you think. It should not take you months to change these things—simply make a decision to think differently! This is true repentance: not just a feeling of guilt or sorrow, but a firm decision to change your mind.

If you do not have close friends, don't sit around feeling depressed and sorry for yourself. First of all, realize that you probably have much better friends than you think you have—especially if you are a disciple already. Satan loves to play tricks on our emotions, convincing us that no one really knows us or cares about us, when in fact we are surrounded by great friends.

Second, decide that instead of waiting for friends to fall into your lap, you are going to do something to change things. Many of us want to be close to people and even have particular people we want to get to know better. Instead of having the courage and vulnerability to seek them out and tell them that we would like to become closer, we hold back, hoping they will come after us. Guess what? This may never happen, and you may completely wish away the opportunity to build a friendship with the person. Don't let fear and pride keep you from initiating with people. The best way to *have* a friend is to *be* a friend.

One of the people who has taught me the most about close relationships is my friend Anne. Shortly after she became a Christian, she found herself feeling very lonely and feeling that no one really knew her. She decided to do something about it. She chose three people whom she wanted to become close to and decided to become one of their closest friends. She started doing the things friends do—she called them, sought to spend time with them and did special things for them to show them how much she cared. Each one of them quickly responded, and she soon found herself with three new best friends!

I would encourage you to do this same thing if you are feeling alone. Don't wait for people to pursue a friendship with you—step out on a limb, and let them know that you want to be close. If they are Christians, you know that they will respond. The truth is, they have probably been wishing they were close to you, and they will be thrilled once you begin to make efforts. Pray for wisdom and ask people you respect for suggestions. Then pick one or two people whom you most want to get to know, deciding to be their friend. This takes some humility and courage, but the rewards are well worth it. If you choose truly spiritual people, you will surely succeed.

Keep in mind the importance of selflessness. Many of us can be self-centered in our friendships and the way we pursue them. We only want to talk about ourselves all the time, and we are only friends with people because of what they can offer us, instead of the other way around. Become a selfless friend. People love to spend time with people who ask a lot of questions about them and who are truly interested in them.

Above all, remember that your confidence and security can never come from people; they must always spring from your relationship with God. Sometimes we want people to be for us what only God can be. We expect the impossible, wanting them to be perfect and to never let us down, but only God can fulfill that role in our lives. People will sin against you. They will become selfish, and they will hurt you at times, even as Christians. It is for this reason that we must allow God himself to be our ultimate source of love, security and friendship.

One last word: Do not withhold your heart from people because you fear getting hurt, even if you may have been hurt in the past. Trust that God will take care of you as you learn to love others as you love yourself (Matthew 22:39).

Whom to Befriend

While God should be our very closest relationship, it is important that we choose wisely those we want to be closest to. Our goal in each of our friendships should be to help one another grow ever closer to God and to become stronger disciples. This goal should naturally lead us to have other Christians as our very best friends. Does that mean we cannot or should not have good friends who are not disciples? Absolutely not! How else will we help people become Christians, if not by befriending them and showing them what Jesus' love and a disciple's life really look like? However, the people with the greatest influence over us should always be other Christians.

One strength I always had growing up and throughout my teen years was in choosing my friends. I was always most attracted to strong disciples, spiritual people with a growing walk with God and deep convictions about righteousness. I wanted friends who would continually call me higher spiritually. Some of my greatest memories are of talks with friends, dreaming about what we wanted to do for God one day and helping one another change our characters and conquer our weaknesses. Those conversations were not forced on us by anyone. They stemmed naturally from our mutual desire to grow spiritually and to please God. It is amazing when we look back now on those times and see how far we have come since those talks.

It is crucial to your spiritual growth that you seek friends who will help you spiritually and not drag you down. Friends have the power to make us stronger as disciples, or to pull us away from God. Teens often value what their friends think above nearly anyone else's opinion, and if their friends are unspiritual, this can be their death warrant as Christians.

As 1 Corinthians 15:33 teaches, "Bad company corrupts good character." I have seen many teens become best friends with weak disciples or non-Christians, and they inevitably pulled one another further and further away from God, until some of them fell away from him altogether. They did not discuss spiritual things with one another and did not expect one another to make changes in their characters. Some were so unspiritually minded that they did not even see one another's spiritual weaknesses. As time went on, they often withdrew further into their own friendship, not allowing anyone else to be close to them or to help them change.

For others, the situation was not quite so dire. Their closest friends were Christians, and they did not lead each other to compromise their convictions in any major way; however they allowed one another to remain complacent spiritually. They laughed and had fun all the time and were content with their current spiritual condition. They allowed one another to be lukewarm, mediocre disciples, never challenging one another. In some ways this condition can be even more scary than the previous one, because it can go undetected for years. People like this are dead weight in the church and the teen group. While others are working hard to advance the kingdom, they remain immature and satisfied, keeping the group from dynamically growing.

There were times when my friends and I realized that we had become somewhat complacent, and every time, we repented quickly. I think part of the reason why God chose to move my family and me to North Carolina after only eight months in New Jersey was to keep me from becoming too comfortable spiritually. The church in North Carolina did not yet have a teen ministry, and I had to rely on my relationship with God in a much greater way than ever before. He wanted to put me in a situation in which I had to grow closer to him, with or without my friends to help me. I was forced to rely much more on my relationship with God, although I must admit that my long-distance phone bills to New Jersey were also quite high during that time! My friends helped to encourage, challenge and disciple me, even from afar.

There were also a number of times in high school when I realized that some of my friends had begun to compromise or slacken spiritually. Some of the most difficult conversations I have ever had were talks in which I challenged them to rekindle their old fire for God. Nothing in me wanted to say those hard things to people I loved, but it was my love and concern for them that drove me to tell them the truth. In the end we were usually much closer.

I had one such conversation with a friend after I had already moved away from New Jersey. He was not yet a disciple, but he was a part of the teen ministry and had been seeking to become a Christian. I had returned for a visit, and as I spent time with him, I was saddened and concerned to see the changes that had taken place in his heart since I had left. He was more distant and aloof from people, more influenced by the world than by Christians and moving rapidly away from God. I was so concerned and upset that I called him shortly before my plane was to leave. I cried as I told him all that I had seen over the past few days, and I challenged him to change his heart. He was stunned, not even realizing how much he had changed, and he too shed tears of sorrow and repentance as he realized the truth of what I had said. That conversation played a key role in helping him to become a Christian in the next few months, and we are still great friends today.

I also had to help Sara when the time came for her to become a Christian. Although she was seeking God, she did not become a disciple for several months after I met her. I still remember the talk we had a few days before her baptism when I had to help her see her sinful nature. I hated doing it and struggled for a long time before getting up the courage to talk to her so forthrightly, but in the end it was a turning point for her that paved the way for her baptism.

In the same way, many of my friends have also had challenging conversations with me over the years to help me become a better, stronger disciple. Those talks may not have been the most pleasant experiences, but I appreciate them for the ways they have changed my life.

Each of us should not only have the desire to strengthen our Christian friends in their walks with God, but also to help all of our non-Christian friends become disciples. If we isolate ourselves from non-Christians and surround ourselves only with Christian friends, we will never accomplish this goal. I had several close friends in high school who were not a part of the church, but each of them knew of my love for God and the convictions I held. Each of them came to visit the church with me on a number of occasions, and several of them even studied the Bible. Although they have not yet become Christians, I still deeply value their friendships, and I will never give up hope for them!

Taking It Deeper

In my early teen years, people used to encourage me to have more spiritual conversations with other teens and to become closer to them. Honestly, I had no idea how to do that. I thought that a deep conversation meant asking someone what they had read in their quiet time that morning! If you need help in knowing how to have more spiritual friendships, start with deepening your own relationship with God. It's easy to talk spiritually when you are continually growing closer to God—you can't help bringing it up. Also, select friends who are genuinely spiritual, and the conversation should take care of itself. If you are still stuck, try doing some of these things:

- *Pray together.* That will bond you as nothing else will.

- *Share victory stories from your life.* Share about the people you are reaching out to.

- *Talk about your greatest dreams, particularly your spiritual ones.*

- *Be honest about your strengths and weaknesses, letting your friend know what you are currently working on in your character.* Help each other with your weaknesses.

- *Discuss Biblical topics*—perhaps what you are studying in your quiet times, or your favorite verses.

- *Talk about your fears.*

- *Share about your family and how you feel about your family relationships.*

- *Share your conversion story.*

Above all, remember that spirituality does not necessarily mean intensity or negativity. You don't have to put on a godly face or be in a godly mood to talk about deep things. Relax, loosen up and have fun. Friendships, especially spiritual ones, should be a blast!

Jealousy,
Competitiveness and Cliques

I think jealousy, competitiveness and cliquishness are at the top of the list of sins that keep teenagers, particularly teen girls, from being close to others. These three sins have been the downfall in many a friendship. Feelings of jealousy and competitiveness were always big struggles for me and really hurt my friendships at different times. I like to be the best at anything I do, and it has often been difficult for me when others have been better than me in any way. I had to learn to celebrate others' victories, enjoying and learning from their strengths, instead of feeling discouraged about myself and jealous of their success.

James 3:14-16 deals with this sin in no uncertain terms:

But if you harbor bitter envy and selfish ambition in your hearts, do not boast about it or deny the truth. Such "wisdom" does not come down from heaven but is earthly, unspiritual, of the devil. For where you have envy and selfish ambition, there you find disorder and every evil practice. (James 3:14-16)

Jealousy is one of Satan's favorite tools for separating people. We must fight this demon in our hearts mercilessly, or risk losing the friendships God has blessed us with. My mom once told me something that has stuck with me and helped me in battling this sin: When we feel jealous, it is for one of two reasons. The first is because either our friend has something that we *should* have (be it a talent, a possession, a characteristic, a friend, or the like), and it is our own fault that we do not have it as well. The second reason we are jealous is because they have something that we *cannot* have, and there is nothing we can do about it.

In the first situation, we should stop feeling jealous, and just do something to change things. This is especially pertinent when dealing with jealousy for a person's accomplishments. Many times, we ourselves could receive the same good grades as our friends, but we are simply too lazy to do so. There is no need to feel jealous of our friends' success. Instead, we should just whip ourselves into shape, spurred on by their example.

In the second scenario, in which we envy things that we cannot have, we must simply accept God's decision and deal with it, or else risk ruining a friendship pointlessly. If your friend has the kind of family you have always wanted, don't be jealous and resentful of her—just be happy for her, and be grateful for the opportunity to spend time with her family. If a friend has beautiful blue eyes and you don't, well—there is nothing you can do about it except get over it!

As I mentioned earlier in this chapter, we also must learn to share our friends with others and not feel threatened whenever they begin to get to know other people. The human heart is an amazing thing—it is capable of loving many different people, and just because it gains a new friend, this does not lessen its ability to love the older ones. Just as a mother is able to love each of her children with all of her heart, and the addition of a new child into the family does not lessen her love for the others, so our friends can get to know other people without losing their special relationship with us. We must learn to be unselfish in our friendships and to include others in them as well. It should not be that three teens can never be close to each other because someone always feels jealous or left out.

In the same way, we must work to never have a clique mentality. Cliques are among the most hurtful things in our teenage years, destroying people's confidence when they feel left out of them. I have seen cliques creep into teen ministry groups on many different occasions, and nothing could be more displeasing to God. He expects absolute unity in his church, and just as he himself never shows favoritism, he expects the same from us (James 2:1-4).

Does that mean we have to be best friends with every single person in our teen ministry? Of course not. There will always be people with whom you hit it off better than others, and there will always be people who want to be your friend but whom you are not extremely attracted to. Our heart should be to love everyone as Jesus did (John 13:34-35) and to make every person feel special and a part of things. We should make a deliberate effort to include everyone in conversations or activities, even if this sometimes requires some sacrifice on our part. Each of us holds responsibility for this—if two or three people remain off to themselves, they can ruin the dynamic and the unity of an entire group.

What about the people who rub us the wrong way, and whom we do not naturally like? I have had to realize that there will always be people whom I do not naturally click with, but this is not necessarily a sin. I need to put into practice the love defined in John 13:34-35 and in 1 Corinthians 13:4-8 with these people. Once I have given them a chance, I have often found out that we had more in common than I thought and have ended up liking them much more. I have learned that love is not a feeling but a decision and an action. It is a way of treating people, regardless of the way you may feel.

A Biblical Precedent

The Bible is replete with examples of incredible friendships—even between teenagers. Perhaps the most famous, and my personal favorite, is the story of David and Jonathan:

> After David had finished talking with Saul, Jonathan became one in spirit with David, and he loved him as himself. From that day Saul kept David with him and did not let him return to his father's house. And Jonathan made a covenant with David because he loved him as himself. Jonathan took off the robe he was wearing and gave it to David, along with his tunic, and even his sword, his bow and his belt. (1 Samuel 18:1-4)

You can read for yourself more about the two teens' relationship in 1 Samuel 19 and 20, and in 23:15-18. They were no different from us, but the two of them forged a friendship that has inspired God's people for thousands of years. They were wholly devoted to one another and strengthened one another in their relationship with God until the day Jonathan died in battle. Theirs is the example to which we can look for inspiration. It is not only possible for teens to tolerate each other and like each other, it is also possible for them to become the best of friends whose influence lasts for years to come.

Treasure the people God has already put in your life. The friends you make as a teenager can remain your friends throughout your life. You may one day be college roommates, serve in one another's weddings, baby-sit each other's children, maybe even plant a mission team for God together—who knows? Give your heart now and when you graduate from high school, you will possess a mountain of memories to cherish for years to come and friendships to last a lifetime.

5. Evangelism

But if I say, "I will not mention him or speak
any more in his name, his word is in my heart
   like a fire, a fire shut up in my bones.
I am weary of holding it in; indeed, I cannot."
JEREMIAH 20:9

"For we cannot help speaking about what
we have seen and heard."
ACTS 4:20

Imagine how you would feel and behave if you somehow discovered a foolproof cure for cancer, if you alone possessed the knowledge and ability to heal millions of sick and dying people around the world. What would your attitude be? You would probably be so excited you'd barely even be able to think straight! You'd want to shout the good news from the rooftops until everyone had heard. People might not believe you at first, and some might dismiss you as deceived or a dreamer, but you wouldn't care what they thought. You would keep spreading the news as fast as you possibly could, because you would know that every moment wasted could mean another needless death at the hands of the awful disease. You would persist in spreading the word, despite hardships and obstacles, even recruiting other messengers as you went along, until every person alive had heard.

Do you realize that as disciples we possess knowledge that far surpasses a cure for cancer? We know the words of life—the way to develop a true relationship with God, to receive absolute forgiveness of sins, and to spend eternity in a place more wonderful than we can even fathom. How do you behave as one possessing such knowledge? Are you desperately attempting to communicate it to everyone possible? The Bible teaches throughout the New Testament that our entire purpose as disciples should be to spread the word about the Bible, Jesus, and the eternal life he provides.

Our attitude should be like that of the Biblical characters in the scriptures quoted at the beginning of this chapter who burned with a ceaseless passion for saving the lost. We too should see where the people around us are headed with their lives and desperately want to save them from that fate. We too must deeply appreciate our own lives and want everyone around us to experience the salvation and joy we have. So many Christians have told me how much they wish they could have become disciples while still in high school. The high school years are the time when many people first begin to face sin in an intense way, and many leave those years with regret and scars that last a lifetime. We have the opportunity to save our friends from the painful plans Satan has for their lives during the high school years and beyond. By sharing our faith with them we can help rescue them from sin and loneliness and offer them a meaningful purpose in their lives, as well.

However, many teens are not as urgent for their friends' salvation as they should be because they are naive about what is really going on in their friends' lives. People say that our generation tends to be shallow, superficial and purposeless, and indeed it does—but look at the families they have all grown up in: A vast majority of our peers have experienced the heartbreak of divorce and remarriage, and it has torn them to shreds emotionally. Their families have been characterized by instability, conflict and conditional love—all of which have produced in them deep feelings of insecurity, loneliness and bitterness. They desperately want to see and experience true, unconditional love, but do not see it modeled anywhere in their lives. They have no idea how to build meaningful relationships with people, much less with their Father in heaven. They therefore seek fun, happiness and fulfillment through shallow venues: popularity, dating relationships, sports, activities and grades. But for many, the high school years remain years of discontentment, restlessness, loneliness, confusion and lingering sadness.

As I have studied the Bible with countless college students, I have gained a sobering view of the sin people become involved in as early as middle and high school. Early on, many have already become intensely bitter toward their parents and families. Most begin sexual experimentation in their early teens. Sadly, I am surprised when I meet a college student who is still a virgin.

I have always tended to be somewhat naive in my view of the world, but in the fall of my junior year of high school, I experienced a shocking awakening. Within a brief two-week span, three students at my high school committed suicide. All three came from well-to-do families living in the best part of town, and one in particular was among the most popular guys at school. Although I had not attended the school long enough to know any of the students who died, their deaths had a profound impact on me. I realized that teenagers—even teenagers belonging to so-called "Generation X"—do think seriously about their lives. They desperately desire to be fulfilled, but the world cannot provide them with the answers and the joy they seek. If we do not urgently spread the news that God is the answer, countless more teens will continue to head unknowingly down the path to spiritual, if not physical, destruction.

God has given you the chance to save your friends from such fates. Do not be deceived by outward appearances of happiness, popularity, innocence or fulfillment. Every one of your friends needs God desperately, and God has put you in their lives for the purpose of helping them know him. Don't underestimate the power of a single conversation or a simple invitation to change the course of someone's life.

While the importance of sharing our faith should weigh heavily upon our hearts, we should not be overwhelmed by it. We cannot walk around in panic mode, terrified that if we do not share perfectly all of our friends may die in an instant—and we will be responsible for their damnation. You must trust that God will protect people whose hearts are open until they hear the message. That trust, while it should not diminish your urgency for them, should keep you from feeling an unhealthy amount of pressure. Once you have shared with a person, do not blame yourself if they do not respond. Your job is just to scatter the seed; only God can actually make it take root in their hearts.

Friendship Is the Key

The best way we can share our faith is by becoming friends with people. Some of us have legalistic notions about evangelism and think that the only way it really counts is if we do something really scary that makes us look like religious freaks. We think we have to always invite strangers to church because unless we feel really uncomfortable doing it, it's not sharing our faith. We picture true boldness as standing on a table in the cafeteria and inviting the entire screaming mob of students to church. While there is certainly a place for doing bold things that challenge and scare us a bit, and for sharing with people we have never met before, the very best way for teens to evangelize is by sharing our lives with those who have become our friends.

I had several close non-Christian friends in high school, and to this day I am still sharing my faith and my life with several of them, hoping that one day they will finally decide to seek God. But I did not limit myself to that small circle of friends. My "group" was continually changing as I sought to find people with hearts that would respond to God. Disciples must fight to transcend the clique mentality prevalent in our schools and make friends with people from every crowd. The best way I found to do this was by being friendly wherever I went, making the most of opportunities to get to know different sets of people in my classes and activities. Become a person who constantly makes new friends and shares your life with them. Some of the people you meet will remain your friends; others may back off a bit when they get to know more about your life and convictions—all the more reason to continually make new friends!

One big mistake that many disciples make is that they isolate themselves from the world, insulating themselves in a spiritual cocoon, surrounded only by friends who are already Christians. While having Christian friends is of tantamount importance, if they are our *only* friends, we will never bring anyone new into God's kingdom. Teens can be especially guilty of religious snobbery. We are so disgusted by the sin we see in people around us that we look down on them and feel they are unworthy to be our friends. We forget that we were once just like them before someone loved us enough to share the truth with us. We can never come off like religious goody-goodies—that attitude will immediately turn people off to God. I had to constantly watch myself so that I did not slip into that mindset. I made a conscious effort *not* to be like all the religious people around me at school. I wanted to stand out as a young woman who had deep convictions about God, the Bible and moral issues, yet was fun and related well to everyone.

Some of us want to share our faith, but do not know how. We make it out to be a terrifying experience reserved only for the ultraspiritual. If you look at evangelism from a friendship standpoint, it loses its terror. When you are friends with people, you cannot help but let them know about your relationship with God and your devotion to him. It's the most important thing in your life, so talking about it should be the most natural thing in the world. Just as it is normal for your family or your boyfriend or your favorite hobby to come up whenever you talk to people, so it should be normal to mention your love for your Father in heaven and your spiritual family.

Get Involved

The best way I found to get to know people at school was by becoming involved in different school activities. At each of my three high schools, I joined clubs or athletic teams. These activities always gave me a group of people to reach out to and to befriend. During my freshman year I served as president of my class, played in the school's concert band and played on the junior varsity basketball team. (That was quite a hilarious experience, since I am by no means built to be a basketball player—my shoes weighed about as much as both of my little stick legs put together!) My sophomore year I participated in the school's theater club and performed in a musical, worked on the staff for a literary magazine, and joined the speech and debate club. My last two years I discovered the activities I really enjoyed when I started running cross country and track, writing for the school newspaper and working with the school's daily news broadcast.

The people I met while involved in these activities became my closest friends at school because we spent so much time together. Many of them have come to church with me throughout the years, and some have even studied the Bible with me. All of my closest friends from high school know about and respect my relationship with God, and we talk very honestly about him. This year I have been amazed to see God bring several people I did not know well in high school back into my life, giving me another opportunity to share my faith with them. I am convinced that God heard all of the prayers I prayed for my high school and that he is still working on many of those people today. I know by faith that it is only a matter of time before someone from my high school becomes a Christian as a college student!

I made a concerted effort to be a part of my school's social life as much as possible. I attended many of the football and basketball games with my friends, attended some of the dances, came to the various school spirit events and attempted to help with our class homecoming float one year. (It flopped horribly when everyone decided to raid another class's float-making party, and our paper-maché creation got rained on and destroyed anyway.) Not only did I have a blast and make incredible memories, but people at school saw me as a normal, fun student and not simply a religious fanatic who stayed at home every night meditating on and memorizing Scripture.

As I mentioned in the chapter on confidence, be careful that you do not become so immersed in school activities that it takes away from your ability to be devoted to God and his church. You are not Superwoman or Superman, and you cannot be involved in every single activity, club and sport at your school!

There were other things I would have enjoyed doing but did not because I did not want anything to interfere with my involvement at church. There were times that I missed some things at school because they conflicted with church or a Bible study, but there was never a question as to what my priority should be. I had to constantly remember the promise in Matthew 6:33: "Seek first his kingdom and his righteousness, and all these things will be given to you as well." Every time I made a sacrifice for God, he honored it by blessing me in unimaginable ways.

Choose a few activities, and devote yourself to them. Decide to be a great example of someone who is on time, responsible, wholehearted and who always has a great attitude.

Making the Grade

Many of us are not fruitful at school because we are terrible examples academically. People do not respect us as students, and therefore have no desire to imitate us spiritually, either. It is imperative that you focus on making the best grades you possibly can. The Bible commands, "Whatever you do, work at it with all your heart, as working for the Lord, not for men" (Colossians 3:23). God does not expect every one of us to be the valedictorian of our class, but he does expect that we give our studies our very best efforts. We should study as if Jesus himself were our teacher! Think about your most recent homework assignments, tests and papers. If Jesus were to take a look at them, would he be proud of your efforts or ashamed? If you are capable of being be a 'B' student, did you turn in 'C' work? If your best efforts should yield 'As,' have you been content with 'Bs'?

We all may have very different academic abilities, so it is impossible to say that every disciple should be expected to make a certain grade point average. However, for many of us the problem with our grades is not our brains, but our discipline. The high school years are an extremely busy time, but if we will develop smart and consistent study habits, we can be successful academically.

Schoolwork was not a tremendously difficult task for me, but I worked very hard in high school. It would have been easy to sit back and coast through my classes, knowing that I would pass the classes simply by putting in a minimal effort. However, I expected to make the very best grades I could, and so I did not settle for half-hearted efforts. As a result, people in my class grew to respect me as a disciplined, hardworking and responsible student. I am convinced that this reputation helped me greatly in sharing my faith. In others' eyes, I had my life together, and so they listened to what I had to say, not only about academics but about God as well.

Our involvement in school or church activities is never an excuse for mediocre academic performance. Some of us may blame God for our poor grades. Shame on you! Becoming a disciple should help you to become a better student, not a worse one. You may have more to juggle in your schedule, but God and God's people can help you to grow in your discipline so that you can handle the challenge. If you are having a difficult time keeping up with your schoolwork and being committed to the church, talk to someone about it and get help immediately. Don't just sit there frustrated; be open! There are many people who can help you come up with a plan so that you can be a devoted disciple and an excellent student at the same time. You may need to reconsider some of the sports or activities you are involved in, adjust your work schedule, or get some tutoring to help you out. There is always a solution, but don't let fear, pride or embarrassment keep you from getting the assistance you need. One of the teen ministry's key responsibilities is helping you to be excellent at everything you do. When you make good grades, you will be far happier, far more confident, and most importantly, far more fruitful for God.

How to Share

Sharing my faith has by no means been easy for me over the years. I worry too much about what people think of me, a weakness that sometimes causes me to hold back from saying all that I should to people. At the same time I sometimes make evangelism a bigger, scarier thing than it should be. I have had to learn how to view it differently and learn how to have great conversations with people.

Our family recently had a devotional time together, and we studied Colossians 4:5-6. Those two verses have really changed the way I view evangelism and have helped me to better understand how I should do it.

Be wise in the way you act toward outsiders; make the most of every opportunity. Let your conversation be always full of grace, seasoned with salt, so that you may know how to answer everyone. (Colossians 4:5-6)

This passage teaches us to be wise in the way we behave toward non-Christians and to take advantage of every opportunity. We should be constantly aware of opportunities to share about anything spiritual, including our life in general, our relationship with God, the church, our Christian friends or even our dates. God provides us with numerous chances to share our faith, but if we aren't paying attention, we will miss them. Verse six teaches us to be aware of the content of our conversations, mentioning the spiritual whenever we can. This doesn't necessarily mean adding "Praise Jesus" at the end of every sentence or even mentioning God directly.

Sharing your faith may not always involve inviting someone to church. Fill your conversations with grace simply by telling someone about a great friendship you have developed at church, or about a fun date you had with a brother or sister at church, about something you have learned recently from events in your life or about a way God has blessed you. You can even share about weaknesses in your life, your own fears, feelings and sins— and how you are learning to deal with them. People are often amazed just by our openness about our lives, which makes them want to know what makes us so different from them.

Seasoning your conversation with salt means that we should share about our convictions whenever possible. Sometimes discussing what you are learning at school can lead to some great conversations in which you share your faith with people and talk about God. Don't be afraid to ask people questions about what they believe, and don't wimp out when given the chance to state your views. I am really attacking this weakness in my life right now and I'm seeking to become a woman known for having strong convictions she is not afraid to share.

This past week has been one of my best weeks evangelistically in a long time. I finally felt like I wasn't simply inviting people to church but that I was sharing my life and my faith with them. And I had so much fun doing it! When we are bold and wholehearted in our evangelism, we are fulfilling the role God intended us to have, and so we are happier and more fulfilled than we ever could be otherwise.

One final note about how to share your faith as a teen: It is of utmost importance that you make every effort to also reach out to your friends' families. Converting teens whose parents are not disciples can be quite complicated unless the parents feel great about the church. I spoke today with a seventeen-year-old who wants desperately to be baptized but whose mother will not allow her to do so. In order to comply with the Bible's command that children respect and obey their parents, she must submit to her mother's desires until she is eighteen and legally an adult. A guy who is close to my brothers has also recently been hindered in his Bible studies because his father has not been supportive of them.

Although we cannot guarantee that even our best efforts will win parents' support, we must do all we can to help them feel great about their teen's interest in God. You will do your friends a huge favor by being a great example to their parents and by having your parents reach out to them (if your parents are disciples). If your parents are Christians, you must work together as a team to share your faith. Invite your friends' families to spend time with your family. They will be amazed by the dynamics of a Christian family, and who knows what could happen in their hearts? The teen ministry in my church recently baptized Susan, a teen woman, and within several months, she baptized her mother and father, as well!

As you think about all these things, be careful not to make sharing your faith more complicated than it needs to be. Sometimes all that is required to change a life is a simple invitation. My dad was a member of a fraternity at the University of Florida. One night he and all the other guys had gathered, waiting for dinner to be served. Dad was going to be moving out of the fraternity house in a couple of months and had been praying fervently to convert some of his fraternity brothers before he left. In all the pre-dinner chaos, Dad noticed a seventeen-year-old freshman standing by himself. Dad did not know the young man well at all but decided to talk to him as he passed by on his way to the dining room. They only talked for a brief moment, but Dad casually invited him to the college devotional at church that night. To this day my dad cannot explain why he did so—devotionals were not supposed to be for visitors! But the student's eyes lit up at the invitation, and he came to devotional that night—and loved it. He began to study the Bible and was dismayed to see that he had never been taught the true way to follow God. Within two or three weeks, he was baptized. Who was the teenager Dad invited to church on a whim? He was Kip McKean, an evangelist whose life and convictions have since touched the lives of thousands around the world!

Confidence No Matter What

One of the biggest struggles that holds teens back in their evangelism is a lack of confidence. Satan knows that if he can get us paranoid about what people think and say about us, get us insecure about ourselves and get us fearful of persecution, he has won. I have already discussed the issue of confidence at length in an earlier chapter, and I urge you to peruse it again if you find yourself still struggling with it. The most important thing to remember is that, as disciples, we are indeed different from the world. There is no way around that fact. We cannot expect to blend in with everyone else. God has set us apart to have an inspiring purpose, and we should never be ashamed of that.

High school has always been one of the most fertile breeding grounds for gossip anywhere in the world. I hate to tell you this, but no matter what you do, no matter who you are, whether you are a Christian or a non-Christian, people are bound to talk about you behind your back at some point. They talk about everyone! So if they're going to talk about you, at least give them something worthwhile to discuss! I'd rather people talk about me because I am a disciple with strong convictions than because I am too shy to ever speak up in class, or because I have no morals and flirt with all the guys. Remember: If they talk about you because you are a Christian, it is because your life challenges them and they feel guilty being around you—not because of anything personal. As difficult as it can be, you must learn to let things people say just roll off your back sometimes. If you don't react, they will eventually get bored and move on to another target.

One of my most victorious moments in high school occurred during my senior year when I was taking a class on politics. The entire class was structured around the debate of various political topics, and the arguments sometimes got pretty heated. The Bible teaches in 2 Timothy 2:24 that "the Lord's servant must not quarrel," so I tried to avoid arguing with people. But I remember there was one day when I had had enough, and I had to speak up. People were debating about what we should do about people who have AIDS and were suggesting absurd things about how we should try to keep them separate from the rest of society so that the disease could not spread any further. They were terrified of contracting the disease, and it never seemed to occur to them that they could avoid the disease by making simple moral decisions about their sexual relationships and intravenous drug use.

I became increasingly saddened and angered by the lack of moral convictions that I kept hearing and raised my hand. I told my class that the solution for AIDS was not quarantining its victims or branding them with the letter 'A,' but getting some morals. If each of them would decide to marry one person and be faithful to them for their whole lives, and keep away from drugs and drug needles, the chances of them contracting the disease would be slim indeed. I spoke with a fervor and passion they had not seen before, suggesting moral ideas that to them were almost revolutionary. As I sat down, they burst into applause.

I had some great conversations with people in that class and was able to share a great deal about the Bible with them. I have never forgotten what it felt like to speak so boldly and confidently, and to realize that students appreciate and respect those who hold high moral standards, even if they do not always adopt those views themselves.

I believe that teenagers are some of the most open people in the world to hearing God's word. Most have not yet become cynical about God or religion, and they have less sin to overcome than others who have been accumulating it for decades. They still possess high ideals and great dreams, and many are searching for truth in their lives. Many of the greatest leaders in God's kingdom today were converted while still teenagers—among them my own parents and many of the world leaders. We have been entrusted with a challenging and precious task, and God will be with us as we strive to fulfill it. Joshua 1:5-6a states a promise from God that I believe holds true for anyone attempting to do his will:

> **"No one will be able to stand up against you all the days of your life. As I was with Moses, so I will be with you; I will never leave you nor forsake you. Be strong and courageous." (Joshua 1:5-6)**

I have shared with countless people in high school and in college, yet only a few have become disciples. Jesus experienced the same thing.

Although he healed and preached to thousands, after his ascension only one hundred and twenty faithful disciples remained (Acts 1). Later on, however, that group became thousands, and those thousands turned their world upside down. We may not always see instant results for all of our efforts, but we can never stop trying. The Bible teaches that our job is simply to plant and water the seed of God's word in people's hearts to help it take root, but only God can actually make it grow (1 Corinthians 3:5-8). We cannot become overcome by guilt if we do not see the results we want to right away; we must keep sharing and persevering until God decides it is time for the seed to grow. It may take mere days, or it may take months or even years before some people respond.

When my family moved to North Carolina, there was no teen ministry in the church here. In fact, I *was* the teen ministry! Being the only teen disciple was sometimes lonely and often discouraging. I prayed for more than two years for him to bring fruit to my high school, but when I graduated, no Christians were left to carry on. But God was still working: The next fall after I graduated, my younger brother David was a freshman there, having recently become a disciple. Over the next three years, that ministry blossomed, and there are now thirteen Christians at that school! Not only that, but the Triangle Church now boasts a teen ministry of more than thirty disciples! God is always faithful and always working, whether we see the results immediately or not. Keep praying and working, and when the time is right, God will answer your pleas in ways you never even dreamed were possible.

6. Emotions

I do not concern myself with great matters
or things too wonderful to me.
But I have stilled and quieted my soul;
like a weaned child with its mother,
like a weaned child is my soul within me.

PSALM 131:1-2

An occurrence when I was three years old may have been the first and only time my parents were ever mildly thankful for my overly dramatic emotions. They took me to see the movie, *Song of the South*, thinking I would be thrilled. But something in the film struck me as being terribly sad, and I began to cry with piercing wails that rose from the depths of my heartbroken young soul. As my guilt-stricken parents drove me home, a policeman pulled them over for driving with an expired inspection sticker. He approached the car and prepared to give them a ticket, but upon seeing me gasping and sobbing in the back seat, he said, "Look, just get this thing fixed, and get that little girl home!"

As I grew older, my emotional pattern continued. I lost my first tooth at the age of five. At first I was delighted at my graduation into the world of adult teeth. But then I began to suspect that the change that had occurred in my mouth was a permanent one, and begged my parents to put the tooth back in. I wept in despair as I realized that my tooth and I had been separated forever.

But my childhood emotions paled in comparison to the challenges I faced once hormones hit. My teenage years were frequently an emotional roller-coaster ride—for me, my family and my friends. I could rarely feel completely happy, as I was constantly battling oppressive feelings of guilt. As I matured somewhat beyond my guilt-ridden years, I faced the emotions of being "in like" and "in love." Every time I came home from college to visit my family, I would either swoon and sigh rapturously as I proclaimed my undying love for the object of my affections—or else I would cry, and declare that I was finally giving up on him. I relate very much to the main character in the movie *Emma,* who passionately declares, "I love John!" but immediately begins to rethink her position and within mere seconds is already sobbing, "I hate John!"

Thank God I am a Christian! If I did not have him in my life to sort me out and get me focused on other people instead of my own feelings, who knows where I would be? I certainly faced my greatest emotional challenges during my teenage years, and it seems that this is the case for most people—particularly for women. Unfortunately, unruly emotions and adolescent girls seem to be inseparable companions. Many of us were already emotional as little girls, but add in a couple of hormones and the challenges of high school, and you've got an explosive mix. We may soar to the heights of ecstasy one moment and plunge to the depths of depression and self-pity the next, leaving our parents, siblings and friends (particularly our male friends!) wondering if we suffer from schizophrenia or manic depression.

While some people do have more serious emotional difficulties that may require the help of a counselor, most of us can gain mastery over our feelings with the help of God, his word and the Holy Spirit.

A Biblical Perspective

God created us with the capacity to experience powerful feelings because he is himself a passionate being. His heart sings in celebration and joy, and swells with love and adoration. At other times he feels sad, angry, frustrated, hurt and abandoned. The Bible says in Genesis 6:6 that God can grieve and that his heart at times is "filled with pain" because of mankind's sin.

He invented the entire gamut of emotions, and as creatures made in his image, we are designed to experience each of those feelings as well. While the Bible does refer often to God as experiencing difficult emotions such as anger or sorrow, he is by nature a supremely happy being. One only has to step outside into the breathtaking glory of his creation to be convinced that he is a God who primarily loves and celebrates life.

What We Should Feel

God knows how emotions are a major influence on our lives, and because of this the Bible provides numerous exhortations about dealing with them in a spiritual way.

> There is a time for everything, and a season for
> every activity under heaven...a time to weep and a
> time to laugh, a time to mourn and a time to dance.
> (Ecclesiastes 3:1, 4)

While every emotion has its proper time and place in our lives, and there are certainly times for mourning and sadness, the Christian experience should overwhelmingly be one of joy, peace and fulfillment. This is not to say that disciples of Jesus lead shallow lives and never face any difficulties; rather, Christians should be able to feel joy and peace in spite of their immediate, challenging circumstances.

The apostle Paul provides a perfect example of the way we should feel about our lives. Although Paul's life was characterized by suffering—he was constantly in and out of prison, flogged, beaten, stoned and lied about, and he was even betrayed and hurt by other disciples—he was one of the happiest people in the Bible. The book of Philippians, which he wrote from jail, is a sublimely joyful book that celebrates the life of a Christian. In it Paul declared:

> I have learned to be content whatever the circumstances. I know what it is to be in need, and I know what it is to have plenty. I have learned the secret of being content in any and every situation, whether well fed or hungry, whether living in plenty or in want. I can do everything through him who gives me strength. (Philippians 4:11b-13)

We cannot allow our emotions to be dictated by our immediate circumstances. So you got a bad grade on a test, or a friend snubbed you, or perhaps your family is going through a difficult period—or maybe you just woke up feeling sad? The Bible teaches us to concentrate on the fact that we are still saved and still members of God's family in spite of everything going on around us, no matter how difficult. In Philippians 4:4 Paul commands, "Rejoice in the Lord always. I will say it again: Rejoice!"

Clearly, it is not an option for us to mope around feeling depressed and discouraged. Paul even says it twice, just in case some of us hardheads don't get it the first time! He even tells us what to do when we are worried. In verses 6 and 7 of Philippians 4 he continues:

> Do not be anxious about anything, but in everything, by prayer and petition, with thanksgiving, present your requests to God. And the peace of God, which transcends all understanding, will guard your hearts and your minds in Christ Jesus. (Philippians 4:6-7)

The key here is prayer. God does not expect us to ignore the difficulties in our lives; he does, however, expect us to pray about them and trust him to take care of them. He promises that once we pray, he will give us a feeling of peace that protects our hearts and minds from discouragement, sadness or faithlessness.

What We Do Feel

These truths may not be new to you. You may have heard them over and over again until you feel you could write this chapter yourself. But sometimes knowing what is right is not enough to change the way we actually feel. Even though I knew all these things to be true throughout my teenage years, and knew that I should be happy and at peace, my unruly feelings were an enormous struggle just the same. At times I just felt sad, sometimes for no reason at all. I often was plagued by a paralyzing sense of guilt, a crushing weight that made me feel lifeless and depressed. Or I felt different and alone—that no one truly knew me or understood what I felt.

I needed a great deal of help to learn how to get my feelings under control and change. I worked on these things throughout my high school years and have still struggled with them as a college student. I am so thankful that God and others have been so patient with me over the years! I still can fall back into old patterns, but I am no longer quite the complicated, confused and extremely emotional person I was for many of my teenage years.

Fact, Fiction, or Feeling?

I am about to tell you one of the most profound spiritual truths I have ever learned: *Feelings are not necessarily the truth.* Shocking, right?

Probably not—most of us at least give some credence to this statement in our heads, yet we do not live as if it is true. We allow our feelings to serve as our spiritual barometer. We determine how well we think we are doing spiritually by how we feel, but we must learn to live by the truth of the Bible instead of our fickle emotions. Just because you *feel* guilty does not mean that you are in sin or that God is furious with you; just because you *feel* lonely at times does not mean you are not close to God or that you have no close friends; just because you *feel* condemned does not mean that you are.

I firmly believe that one of Satan's favorite weapons against teenage women is their emotions. One crazy feeling can send them into a tailspin from which they do not recover for days, weeks or months. There is a time to listen to our feelings and to take them seriously, but each of us must learn to distinguish between unfounded feelings and truth. Emotions can be groundless, irrational and even simply the product of whacked-out hormones. We must learn to treat some of them as such. I have had to train myself to believe the Bible and spiritual people instead of my own emotions. Even the strength of a feeling does not confirm it as definitely true.

The best way I know to take hold of my emotions is by becoming a truly spiritual woman. I delved deeply into the Bible to answer my questions. For example, I studied out the subjects of guilt, the love of God, joy, and having a spiritual mindset all through my teenage years until I gained a more godly understanding of them. I now have an arsenal of scriptures to which I can turn whenever my emotions start to overwhelm me.

I also sought a great deal of help from spiritual people around me. I talked about my feelings continually, and people were able to help me determine which emotions were real and which were unjustified. I think I must have driven my mother to near insanity at times. It felt like we had the same conversation over and over again every two weeks or so. I would come to her confessing all my feelings of guilt, she'd patiently talk me through them, and I would feel better...for about two weeks, that is, and then we would repeat the same cycle all over again!

It is crucial that you open up about your feelings with other Christians. Many of us feel isolated and guilty because we think we are the only people on the planet who feel as we do. Talking about our feelings solves that problem right away because we quickly realize that others have thought and felt the same way. Part of Satan's plan is to isolate you from other people by convincing you that you alone think and feel the bizarre things that you do.

Changing Your Mind

My dad, another complicated thinker who feels things every bit as passionately as I do, has taught me repeatedly that our emotions are the product of our thoughts. For example, if we concentrate all day on our sins and how awful we are, then of course we are going to feel guilty and depressed! Dad continually encouraged me to change my feelings by changing my mind. I had to set my mind on what God wanted me to think about. Verses like the ones following helped me to figure out what God wants us to focus on:

> **Finally, brothers, whatever is true, whatever is noble, whatever is right, whatever is pure, whatever is lovely, whatever is admirable—if anything is excellent or praiseworthy—think about such things. (Philippians 4:8)**

Since, then, you have been raised with Christ, set your hearts on things above, where Christ is seated at the right hand of God. Set your minds on things above, not on earthly things. For you died, and your life is now hidden with Christ in God. (Colossians 3:1-3)

A song of ascents. Of David.
My heart is not proud, O Lord,
  my eyes are not haughty;
I do not concern myself with great matters
  or things too wonderful for me.
But I have stilled and quieted my soul;
  like a weaned child with its mother,
  like a weaned child is my soul within me.

O Israel, put your hope in the Lord
  both now and forevermore. (Psalm 131:1-3)

God wants us to fill our minds with spiritual thoughts—of him, of his Son and of his purpose for our lives. Many of us spend our days thinking about how sinful we are or wishing we had a different life, a better life. Instead of resting securely and thankfully in God's care, at peace in our hearts and minds, we try to analyze every little detail. We spend hours trying to figure out God's plan for our own lives, the lives of everyone around us, even the whole world. No wonder we're depressed and overwhelmed!

It is not our job to figure out how the world should be run, or even how the lives of our friends and family should go. As Psalm 131 says, we should not concern ourselves with the unfathomable. When I was a child,

I would sometimes start worrying needlessly about things that were my parents' concern. My mom would always tell me, "You just let me be the mommy, and you be the little girl." Some of us need to relax, let God be the Daddy in charge, and let ourselves just be the little kids.

Our mindset should be positive as we continually remember all of our blessings. It's hard to feel guilt-ridden and depressed when we are constantly meditating on how great God is and how much he has loved and blessed us.

Once we have firmly decided to think about the things God would have us think about, we can and must decide what we will feel. Believe it or not, you can decide to be happy and to be at peace! There was a time when I thought this was impossible, but God has proven me wrong once again. We do have control over our emotions, especially once we have the Holy Spirit in our hearts.

Breaking It Down

There are certain emotions that seem especially effective at entrapping teenagers, and I have found that I need to take a different approach in dealing with each one. What are these particular emotions, and how should we handle them?

Guilt

So many disciples are overwhelmed by feelings of relentless guilt. They think that they must be flawless and that they must repent perfectly of all their sins before they can be close to God. News flash: None of us is perfect! If we were, we'd be named "Jesus," and we'd be hanging out with God in heaven right now! This seems like such an elementary revelation, but it has taken me years to understand it. We all sin more times a day than we'll ever know, but this is why we are *in* Christ. His blood continually washes over us, cleansing and forgiving us, even when we do not realize it is at work. The *only* way we could ever forfeit that forgiveness is by deliberately walking away from God.

We must learn to relax and enjoy living by grace. We must be confident that if we are disciples, we are absolutely going to heaven, flaws and all. We certainly do not deserve such blessings, and we may never understand why God has so generously poured them out on us, but that's okay—our job is to enjoy them and to love him in return. It's really that simple.

Repentance:

Although repentance is not a feeling, I include it here because many of us confuse repentance with an emotional experience. We think that every time we sin, we are supposed to conjure up a deep, tearful sadness and feelings of remorse. But Biblical repentance actually has little to do with emotion—it is simply a decision to change. You must realize that you are in sin and decide to head in the opposite direction. Sometimes we may not even feel an enormous sense of regret. We just need to change and be different.

Yes, it is often appropriate for us to experience a godly sorrow for our sins, but God does not expect us to wallow around for several weeks in a pit of despair, flogging ourselves and sobbing in sorrow. If we all did that, we would spend the rest of our days in a puddle of tears because we have new sins to repent of several times a day! You may want to study 2 Corinthians 7:8-11 to give you an idea of the difference between healthy, godly sorrow and worldly sorrow.

Depression:

Sadness and depression are feelings that haunt many people throughout their teenage years. Sometimes we can attribute them to specific incidents in our days or situations in our lives, but sometimes such emotions attack us with no warning and no obvious causes. They enslave and smother us until we feel there is no way we can ever feel happy again. Although some people do have more serious emotional challenges that may require professional help, I know that many mature leaders believe that the vast majority of us can conquer depression with the help of God and the Bible. I remember many days when I woke up simply feeling sad and I had no idea why. I have had to learn to master those feelings because my only other option is to give in to them and allow them to run my life.

When I start to feel depressed, I first determine whether or not there is a specific cause for my emotions. Sometimes I need to resolve a conflict with a friend or confess and repent of some sin. This done, I spend a few minutes praying, and I firmly decide to give my feelings over to God. I pray for his forgiveness if I have sinned, and ask for his help. Then I resolve to set my mind on something different. It is best for me to immediately busy myself so much with giving to other people that I do not have time to think much about how I feel.

I realize that my feelings will rarely change as soon as I stop praying—our feelings operate much the same way our stomachs do when we eat. Just as it often takes us about twenty minutes of eating before we realize that we feel full, so it sometimes takes our emotions twenty minutes or so to catch up to the decisions we have made! In the meantime, I don't sit around waiting for a different emotion to wash over me. I move on, act differently and just forget about my feelings altogether. Later on, I usually am surprised to find myself feeling much better.

There are times when feelings of sadness persist, even though I have done all these things, and this is when I have to fight even harder. In those cases Satan is simply toying with my feelings and trying to distract me from my purpose. I must tell him to get lost. I immerse myself in giving to other people and decide not to take my feelings seriously. I refuse to give Satan the satisfaction of seeing my day ruined by his games.

Loneliness:

One of the most common complaints I hear from teenagers is that they do not feel deeply close to people and that they feel lonely. Loneliness may strike at the oddest times—while walking to class, while watching two people laugh together, while lying in bed. Many of us need to realize that we have closer friends than Satan would have us believe. Although some of us do need help in learning how to become close to people and how to talk openly with them about our lives, those of us who are disciples usually have many people who know and love us. Don't let Satan convince you that you have no friends when in fact you are surrounded by them!

You may indeed need to get help in becoming closer to people, but it is even more important that you feel close to God. People will never be perfect and will never know or understand everything about us; only God can do that. No one understood Jesus or sympathized with his mission; however, he relied on God to be his closest friend. He spent all his time serving others in spite of their failings.

Sometimes we also need to realize that we feel lonely because we are selfishly waiting for others to come to us and give to us. We must decide to stop feeling sorry for ourselves, and go be a great friend to someone else. It's hard to feel lonely when you are constantly giving to people.

Insecurity:

Insecurity is a biggie, so big in fact that I devoted an entire chapter to it! See the chapter on confidence for an in-depth look at how we can overcome feelings of insecurity and become confident men and women of God.

There is no way I could provide an in-depth analysis of how to deal with every emotion we experience, but I hope that the principles you see here will assist you in dealing with whatever emotional challenges you may face. The teenage years can simultaneously be the best and worst years of your life—the time when you attain the greatest highs and sink to the lowest depths. It is best for you to mature to the point of being consistent and stable, not fluctuating from one extreme to the other.

Dealing with emotions is by no means an easy task. I believe it is one of the most difficult battles many of us face throughout our Christian lives—no matter how old we are. Above all, be extremely patient with yourself as you tackle these issues. Realize that you will have awesome times and horrible times, sometimes within minutes of each other! Learn to celebrate and savor your victories. Use those times to bolster your confidence for the next battle. If you have a bad day, so what? Pick yourself up and start fighting again. You may have lost a minor battle, but remember that because you are a Christian, Jesus has already won the war for you.

While it is important to be patient with yourself and not expect perfection immediately, this is not a license to remain an emotional basket case. We can never allow our feelings to be an excuse for sin in our lives or a weakness we tolerate because we think we "cannot help it." It is sinful and disrespectful to God if we continually allow ourselves to be dominated by unrighteous feelings and do not strive wholeheartedly to change. It is one thing to battle with complicated feelings; it is another to give in to them after feeble or halfhearted efforts. It deeply wounds God when, having heard what we must do to change, we refuse his solutions and his grace, stubbornly wallowing in loneliness, faithlessness and depression.

My twentieth birthday was a milestone of sorts in my life. Not only did it mark the end of my teenage years, but with it I felt I was leaving behind many of the emotional struggles with which I had wrestled in adolescence. When my mom called me that morning to wish me a happy birthday, I thanked her for putting up with me during my teen years. We both laughed as we thought about how much I had grown and changed. I still face the challenges of dealing with complicated feelings, but they do not enslave me as they did for so many years. Even when I am attacked by guilt or discouragement, I can conquer my feelings fairly quickly.

I am convinced that every disciple can have similar victories over their emotions. With God's help, we do not have to remain fickle, weak or helpless. Don't you dare let Satan convince you otherwise. If he knocks you down one day, pop back up again and hit him right back! Let us take on the fighting spirit of Paul, who strove even as an old man to become more like Jesus and to conquer his sin:

> But one thing I do: Forgetting what is behind and straining toward what is ahead, I press on toward the goal to win the prize for which God has called me heavenward in Christ Jesus. (Philippians 3:13b-14)

My prayer is that you too will fight the battle of emotions with all your heart, leaving your failures in the past and straining with all your might to become the most powerful disciple you can possibly be!

7. Relationship with Parents

Children, obey your parents in the Lord, for this is right. "Honor your father and mother"—which is the first commandment with a promise—"that it may go well with you and that you may enjoy long life on the earth."

EPHESIANS 6:1-3

"Obey your parents" is one of the ten commandments given by God to Moses and the Israelite nation, and the first commandment to offer a blessing to those who adhere to it. God promises that if we honor, respect and love our parents, we will have great lives that endure for many years. The Bible is absolutely clear on the relationship between parents and their children. Children are to honor, respect and love their parents, and parents are to love, discipline and train their children.

The teenage years are notoriously the time when many teens begin to really rebel against their parents for the first time. Suddenly, they feel as if their arrival at adolescence has made them so brilliant, experienced and even spiritual that they can discern what is best for their own lives. They think they know better than their parents do. Teenagers' complicated emotions don't help at all—and unless both the teens and the parents are spiritual, adolescence can be a time that severely damages or even destroys these relationships.

Honoring Our Parents

When God commands us to honor our parents, it means that we should love and respect them with all of our hearts. We should listen very carefully to them, be obedient to them and genuinely admire them. Children should be their parents' biggest fans!

When I was three and four years old, I loved the television show, *The Incredible Hulk*, which stars an extraordinarily muscular, green monster. One day I walked up to my dad and permanently won his affections by declaring, "Daddy, the Incredible Hulk is big like *you* are!"

Many of us had this respect and admiration for our parents when we were younger but have lost it. We are either too critical of them to see anything good in them, or we are too prideful to admit how much we really do respect them. I talked about my parents to my high school friends all the time, and they were amazed to hear about the relationship that we had. They thought it was really cool, and some of them were jealous! Perhaps my proudest moment in high school was when my father was able to speak at my Baccalaureate ceremony before graduation.

If you have not already figured this out, let me clue you in on a mind-boggling fact of life: Your parents are not perfect. They, like you, are sinners! Many of us have completely unrealistic expectations for our parents. You may have thought that they were perfect when you were a child, and you still expect them to be perfect now. There is not a perfect parent anywhere on the planet. Give your parents a break, and let them be normal human beings with weaknesses just like you. They are going to mess up, hurt your feelings and say stupid things to you or to each other, but this is all part of life.

Even though our parents are imperfect, God still commands us to honor them absolutely. As we mature and begin to see flaws in our parents, we must make decisions about how we will respond. Many teens handle this realization by choosing to become critical and ultimately losing respect for them. They may even rebel outright. They feel that God's laws about respect only apply when the parents in question are perfect or sinless (and also nonexistent)!

Just seeing sin or weakness in your parent can be quite a shocking and unsettling experience. I remember some of the times when I realized that my parents had weaknesses and sins just as I did—and that we actually share many of the same sins! I didn't know what to think or feel. Part of me felt scared by the realization, part of me felt guilty, and then another part of me became critical of them at times. It is not wrong to notice that our parents have weaknesses, and even to feel hurt by their sins. It is very wrong if we hold our parents' weaknesses and failings against them and become critical and judgmental of them.

I did not initially deal well with the realization that my parents were imperfect. Instead of having the same kind of mercy on them that they have had on me throughout my entire life, there were times when I criticized them and held their sins against them. I especially had to deal with this in my relationship with my mom. Adolescent girls tend to struggle at times in their relationships with their moms. Many of us can be "daddy's girl" but have real problems with our mothers. This stems from pride, competitiveness and insecurity, all rolled up in one ugly package.

There were several times that I deeply hurt my mom because of critical feelings I confessed to her. I cringe even writing this, because I now realize how arrogant, hypocritical, ungrateful and unmerciful that was of me. My mother was the one friend I had throughout my rough years as a young teen, loving and forgiving me when I was an absolute jerk. She had been patient with me when other people would have written me off as a complicated, annoying head case. Yet when I saw little things in her, I became critical and judgmental. Who did I think I was? Even now it brings tears of anger and regret to my eyes when I remember having those feelings and thoughts.

It is disgusting to God when he sees us behave like that. In fact it infuriates him. In Deuteronomy 21:18-21, God commanded the Israelites under the old covenant to have the elders stone to death any rebellious, arrogant children! If you have allowed yourself to harbor critical, resentful or judgmental thoughts toward your parents, you must repent of these thoughts immediately. Confess them to someone who can help you, and apologize to your parents with all your heart.

I remember weeping as I told my mom how sorry I was for my arrogant behavior, and writing her cards to let her know just how much she meant to me. I spent extra time in my quiet time thanking God for all the wonderful things I saw in my mom, and even wrote all those things down for myself so I could fully realize what an incredible woman she is. The most amazing thing I saw in her was her willingness to forgive me so completely, even when I had hurt her. Because she was forgiving and did *not* treat me as I had treated her, our relationship was quickly restored, and we once more became the best friends we had always been before.

If you are realizing as you read this that you need to repent of attitudes toward your parents, I encourage you to deal with them quickly. Don't allow another day to go by in which you are not close to your parents (as you need to be).

Just one other thing about respecting your parents: Ask yourself what you sound like when you talk to your parents. Some of us speak to our parents in the most appallingly disrespectful ways—even as Christians. We whine, complain and argue. We are sarcastic and obnoxious; we are know-it-alls who dismiss every word that our parents say as absurd and outdated. Taking these tones with our parents is absolutely sinful, and should never emerge from our lips to anyone, under any circumstances, least of all to our parents. Some of you would never speak to your friends, or even your teachers, the way that you speak to your parents—and this is completely displeasing to God. If you are not sure whether or not you do this to your parents, ask them—they'll tell you! Or ask your siblings or your friends (friends who will tell you the truth) how you come across.

Honoring Is Obeying

Another key way that we must honor our parents is by obeying them. God commands obedience, as we have already seen in Ephesians 6:1. Colossians 3:20 reads, "Children, obey your parents in everything, for this pleases the Lord." Does he say we should only obey when we like what is being said, or when it is convenient for us, or when we can still look cool just like all our friends? Nope! It says that we should obey our parents in *everything*—whether it be concerning a curfew, whether or not we are allowed to date, or where we are allowed to go with our friends.

The teenage years are an awkward time, because we have more freedom to make decisions about our lives, and there are many more options open to us. Many of us can drive, we are old enough to be interested in dating, we have some say in the classes we take, we can choose whether or not to play sports or be involved in clubs, and most importantly, we can make our own decisions about our relationship with God.

Adolescence is an exciting time, but it is also the time when many people abuse their new freedom and end up sinning very seriously—and in that sense, it can be a scary time! You may feel so old and mature once you hit high school, but you must realize that there is a lot in life that you have absolutely no clue about. Even though your parents went through adolescence many years ago and probably wore some really ugly clothes at the time, they still know a great deal more than you do about making it through adolescence. Let them help you! They are not out to ruin your life when they make suggestions or lay down rules for you. They are simply trying to protect you. It might not be fun to have an earlier curfew than all of your other friends, or to not be allowed to date yet, but instead of resenting your parents, you should appreciate how much they love you and are concerned for you! I know very few parents who make rules just for the twisted pleasure of ruining their teenagers' lives.

And guess what? In the same way that adolescence is a new experience for you, so it is also a new experience for your parents! You've never been a teenager before, and they've never dealt with you as a teenager before, either—so none of you knows exactly what to expect. They are probably scared to death! All of a sudden, you look more like an adult, you act more like an adult, you have hormones and crazy emotions that make you cry at the drop of a hat, and—heaven forbid—you are attracted to the opposite sex! You were much easier to deal with when you were a young child, and now they have no idea of how to deal with you. If you are the oldest child in your family, like I am, they *really* don't know what to do with you. If you're a girl, their first instinct is probably to lock you up in the house all day long where you can't get into any trouble, nobody can mess with you or hurt your feelings, and no boys can come after you! So, hey—if you get to go out at all, even if your curfew is 7:00, you're doing pretty well, and you should thank your parents big-time! If you aren't allowed to date but are allowed to at least speak to guys, be thankful that your dad isn't standing guard outside your house all day long with a shotgun—this is a big step for him.

I know I am joking around a little here, but seriously, we have to understand that adolescence is a new thing to our parents, too. And since they're not perfect, sometimes they'll mess up—just as we will. So be patient, and let them learn, just the same way you expect them to be patient with you as you grow up. If they are a little overprotective, don't resent it. That just proves that they care deeply about you and want to protect you from getting hurt.

My parents have always been a little more protective than some of my friends' parents, but I really appreciate that. I feel so loved and cared for. They always encouraged me to get in bed at reasonable hours, and whenever I went out, we agreed upon a time when they could expect me back so that they would not worry. I was not allowed to ride in a car unless I was wearing a seat belt, which was a very good thing, considering the way some of my friends drove in high school! Even now, I am a 21-year-old college junior, but my parents still worry about me and tell me what to do at times. When I go home for the summer and Christmas holidays, I still try to be in by a decent hour so they don't worry, and I still check with them before I make plans.

If you prove yourself to be obedient and trustworthy, your parents will probably give you more and more freedom as you get older. I was allowed to do many things by my senior year in high school that I never could have done as a freshman. Don't spend high school fighting with your parents and making your lives miserable. Just decide to be a great daughter or son no matter what.

Also, don't let yourself off the hook by just obeying your parents grudgingly—doing what they say, but rolling your eyes, making faces, sighing despondently, slamming doors, or stomping off in a huff as you do it. That's so immature. Grow up and get out of preschool! Consider Paul's words in Philippians 2:14-15:

> Do everything without complaining or arguing, so that you may become blameless and pure, children of God without fault in a crooked and depraved generation, in which you shine like stars in the universe. (Philippians 2:14-15)

So what about if your parents ever tell you to do something that you feel is wrong? What does God think about that? It really depends on the situation. God would never have us break his commands because of what another person tells us to do, but few of us ever encounter a situation in which our parents actually command us to sin. Sometimes we may not like what they tell us, but often that is just a matter of opinion, not of right and wrong. If something your parents ask you to do violates your conscience before God, then you need to first pray for wisdom, and search it out in your Bible to see if there is a Biblical command about it. You can humbly mention your concern to your parents, and ask them to help explain their thoughts about the matter to you. This should clear up most issues that you may have. If they are Christians, then they probably have a good explanation for why they are thinking as they are. If you still feel unresolved about the issue after talking with your parents, or if it is a particularly sensitive issue, you may need to seek some advice from another Christian. I would recommend talking to someone like your discipler or one of the teen workers at church. They can help you decide what the wisest approach would be to your particular situation.

Honoring Is Openness

Teens tend to have the bizarre idea that once they hit adolescence, they should no longer be close to their parents, because it's not cool and because their parents probably wouldn't understand them anyway. What a stupid idea! Whoever thought of it should be flogged or something. Our teenage years are a time when, because we are older, we actually have more in common with our parents than ever before. These are the years when you can have not only a parent-child relationship, but you can truly become friends.

Although we had bumps here and there, my relationship with both my parents during high school was characterized by a deep closeness and best friendship. As I have grown older, we have become even closer (which was hard to imagine!), building on the groundwork we laid at that time. My mom and I can talk to each other for hours on end and not become bored. Whenever I go home, I have to make rules for myself about not going downstairs until I have read my Bible and prayed. Otherwise, Mom and I will spend the entire morning talking, and I'll miss my time with God! We talk about everything—from our relationships with God, to our dreams, to the details of my dating life. It's so much fun, and I have learned so much about life, God and the ministry just by hanging out with her.

In the same way, my dad and I have such a special relationship, unlike any other in my life. He is my hero of all time, and the model for the kind of man I want to marry. We share so many of the same passions and can understand each other's interests in even the seemingly most insignificant things. We recently had an opportunity to spend an unexpected morning together while I was home for spring break, and we had an absolute blast! In a matter of about thirty minutes, we discussed everything imaginable—from our mutual passion for writing and history, to politics, to the history of God's kingdom. When we returned home, we both teared up as we talked about how much we just loved being together.

Please open up your heart to your parents. Let them be your friends. Don't put on a stupid act in which you pretend not to need them. Be humble and vulnerable, and let them know the real you. Talk about your feelings, thoughts and struggles. Your parents can help you so much at this time in your life, and most of them really want to be close, but so many times it is the teenagers who refuse to allow them into their hearts. Consider the admonition of Paul:

> We have spoken freely to you, Corinthians, and opened wide our hearts to you. We are not withholding our affection from you, but you are withholding yours from us. As a fair exchange—I speak as to my children—open wide your hearts also. (2 Corinthians 6:11-13)

Open wide your heart, and let your parents in. Remember that love is not a feeling, but a decision and an action. Don't wait for your feelings to be just right before you act—do what you know is right, and God will work on your emotions as you go.

What about those whose parents have not made efforts to become as close as they would like to be? There are certainly many teens who would love to be close to their parents, but do not feel they can be because their parents are not warm, loving or receptive. My own father had a very difficult time getting close to his dad. His dad had a great sense of humor and really loved all of his children, but he also had a bad temper that scared my dad. He died when my dad was only twelve, and they never had the chance to build the kind of relationship my dad had always wanted. My dad felt hurt and deep regret for many years, until he learned to allow God to be the father he needed, and until he was able to remember all the ways his father had sought a close relationship with my dad in his own way. Imperfect people can never substitute for God's role in our lives—only he can provide us with the security and unconditional love we need.

If you have a difficult time getting close to one or both of your parents, don't be discouraged by that. You are certainly not alone! It may be that you need to change a lot in yourself, and it may also be that your parents have not made the effort they should have made to be close to you. If this is the case, study how Jesus treated people who treated him unjustly and unkindly, and look at how much he loved them in spite of their actions. It will not be easy by any means, but it may be that if you would take the first step in seeking a closer relationship, or in making yourself vulnerable to them, you may be able to break through some of the barriers that separate you from each other. You have to start somewhere, so don't be discouraged if things don't change right away. It may be that your parent or parents never knew how to be close to their own parents, and so they honestly don't know that things should be any different.

Honoring Is Gratitude

So many of our problems with our parents could be solved if we would simply appreciate our parents and all that they do for us. Teens are notoriously ungrateful for all the blessings in their lives, but especially for their parents. Your parents are imperfect and have surely done innumerable things wrong. They have probably even hurt you at times. Even if your parents are not expressive and have not made all the efforts they should have to be close to you, God expects you to appreciate them.

I encourage you to do something this week to let your parents know how much you appreciate them, and to do such things often. Write a card, give a gift, give a hug or just tell them in person.

Even if you don't feel thankful right away, expressing your gratitude has a way of making you feel it more strongly. If you struggle with criticizing your parents or if you have a hard time being close to them, then you especially need to do this! Take some special time to write down for yourself all the things you appreciate about your parents, and keep that list so that you can look at it whenever you are tempted to have a bad attitude or simply take them for granted. It will do you a lot of good and will probably transform the way you view them.

Kingdom Kids

This discussion of gratitude leads me into a very important area, and I want to address "kingdom kids" for a moment—those of you who have grown up in the kingdom of God with Christian parents, and especially those of you whose parents have been leaders in God's church.

We are some of the most fortunate people alive. Most of us have absolutely no idea how blessed we really are to have been raised as we have. Having Christian parents is, besides salvation itself, the greatest blessing God could possibly give us. We are spared so much of the heartache and suffering that everyone around us endures. We were born with salvation sitting in our laps, waiting for us to pick it up. Our parents are godly, spiritual people who have raised us the way God would want us to be raised.

We should therefore be the most grateful people alive. Not a day should go by when we do not thank God for the life we have led. Yet I am sad and ashamed to say that we are often the people who appreciate God's kingdom the least. We act as if we deserve salvation and special treatment, when we should be falling all over ourselves searching for ways to serve and show our appreciation.

I have definitely been ungrateful many times for my parents and my life in the kingdom. As I have seen more of the world and studied the Bible with countless women who did not have a family or life like mine, I have come to appreciate it so much more. I am in awe that God chose me to have the family I have and the life I have had thus far. I would not trade it for anything or switch places with anyone.

While we need to grow in our gratitude and continually remind ourselves how blessed we are, we should not feel guilty because of the life we have had. Some of us can feel so unworthy and can beat ourselves up in an effort to try to deserve what we have—and sometimes other disciples can make us feel guilty, because they wish so much that they had the same opportunities we have had. There is absolutely no reason to feel guilty for our lives. We should simply be overflowing with gratitude and should let that thankfulness compel us to share our faith that much more. We cannot give other people our childhood or our family, but we can tell them about what life is like when God comes first in a family. We should be the most evangelistic people in the kingdom!

We can also be unselfish with our families, enabling them to help others. My family loves it when any of us brings a friend home, and our friends are invariably amazed at the love in our home. A number of people have become Christians after seeing God's power at work in the relationships within our family. Other disciples, particularly other students who have grown up in families that are not close, are similarly amazed and inspired by spending time with our family. We serve as their family if they do not have a close one of their own, and they catch a vision for what they can one day build for themselves.

One final thought to kingdom kids: If you are especially close to your parents, that is great, and something you should be proud of and thankful for. However, it cannot be that you only allow your parents to disciple you. You must allow other people into your life to train and help you spiritually and not allow your relationship with your parents to serve as an excuse for being independent from others whom God wants to use in your life.

Being in the campus ministry was a challenge for me my first year, because it was the first time when I had ever really let anyone besides my parents into my life. I had to learn to be humble and to accept advice, challenge and help from other disciples and not go running home to my parents all the time. My parents are an incredible help to me, but I had to decide that they would not be a spiritual crutch for me. I desperately need other people in my life as well, people who are a bit more objective than my parents and who may have a different view of things.

I have had to learn that other people may even do things differently than my parents do, but this is not necessarily bad. My parents do not know everything (nor do they claim to!), but it would be foolish for me to limit myself only to their opinions in my life. I appreciate having many different points of view to help me to grow spiritually.

Non-Christian Families/ Challenging Family Situations

Some of you reading this may be having a hard time knowing what to do with it because your parents either are not disciples or because you have a difficult family situation. Perhaps your parents are divorced and you only live with one parent, or you have one or more stepparents, or perhaps you have never even met one or both of your parents.

These can indeed be very challenging and sometimes very hurtful situations. There is no way that I can list all the possible family situations you may be involved in and provide specific advice, but I can tell you some principles to keep in mind. The most important thing you must do is believe with all of your heart that God has an amazing plan for your life and that he has called you to follow him at a young age for that very reason. His goal is for you to be around Christian families while you are still in high school, so that one day you will know how to build an awesome Christian family of your own. You must also remember that your security and your source of unconditional love must be God, not your parents. Some people spend their entire lives unhappy, insecure and unfulfilled because they do not feel loved by or close to their parents. As I suggested in the chapter on having a relationship with God, read everything you can in the Bible about God being your father, your caretaker and your shepherd.

If your parents are not Christians, it is crucial that you help them to feel great about your involvement with the church. That responsibility falls primarily on your shoulders, not on those of the teen workers or other disciples in the church—although they do need to help you in whatever way they can. If your parents are open to the idea, set up times for them to spend time with Christian parents of other disciples. It will help your parents to feel good about the church if they see that other parents also want their teens to be a part of the church. That way, adult disciples will have an opportunity to share with your parents and perhaps help them become Christians themselves!

At my old high school, a girl named Susan, whom I mentioned before, was recently baptized after being reached out to by one of the guys in the teen ministry. She brought her parents to church, and they loved it. They became friends with some of the married couples at church and began to study the Bible as well. Within a few months, both of her parents became Christians. Her dad shared at his baptism that the thing that helped him the most was seeing the lives and relationships of the teen disciples.

Regardless of whether or not your parents are supportive of your involvement in the church, you must be especially careful to be very responsible. You have a responsibility before God to set a great example at home, not to preach at your family or tell them that they are going to hell, but to be a great servant, daughter and sister. Your family should be amazed by your attitude—especially by the way you serve.

Be very careful always to communicate very clearly with your parents about your attendance at church-related functions. Be responsible about finding rides, and always be home when you say you will. If your parents feel that you are reliable and responsible, they will be far less likely to prevent you from being involved. If a situation ever arises when your parents do not want you to attend something at church, be very wise in the way you handle it. Do not pout and make a scene. You can humbly and calmly let them know what you would like to do and why, but then you have to let it go. Trust that God is in control, even of situations like that.

Another thing that would be very helpful is for you to keep the teen workers in touch with your parents. Your parents need to know the people who look after you at church so that they can trust them. It would help to even have a friend who works in the teen ministry spend time hanging out at your house every once in a while, just so your parents can get to know them. Your parents have a right to be concerned about who you spend your time with. Also, let your parents get to know your friends in the teen ministry. They will be impressed by your friendships and will want you to remain friends with such respectful, responsible teens.

Your high school years will fly by before you even know it. A class period may seem to last an eternity, but do not be deceived. Just as you finally feel you've gotten the hang of being a student—you've figured out your way around school, you've learned all the cool slang, figured out where to sit at lunch, and more importantly, you've gained confidence and conviction as a disciple—it will be time to order your cap and gown.

These four years will most likely be the last ones you will spend at home with your parents. They are such a special time, a time that will never come again, no matter how much you may want them to. One day soon you will pack off for college, and your life will change for good. You will still have your parents, but it will not be quite the same. You won't be able to run downstairs every morning to get one of your dad's bear hugs, or go grocery shopping with your mom, talking and giggling the whole time. Do not squander this time. Draw close to your parents now; spend the extra time with them now; open your heart now. Then when you move on to college and the rest of your life, you will look back with tears in your eyes, treasured memories in your heart and the kind of relationships that will only grow closer and richer in years to come.

Epilogue

Now to him who is able to do immeasurably more than all we ask or imagine, according to his power that is at work within us, to him be glory in the church and in Christ Jesus throughout all generations, for ever and ever! Amen.

EPHESIANS 3:20-21

It is amazing how much God can change in your life in just eight months! When I finished writing the chapters of this book, I was a twenty-one year old junior at Duke University. Now here I sit, two days away from my twenty-second birthday, a Duke graduate, working full-time for God's church, and engaged to be married to the man of my dreams in less than four months! As if that weren't enough, my lifelong dream of publishing a book is about to come true.

As I have indicated before, I do not deal well with change, and I remember being concerned at my high school graduation that maybe the glory days were over. After all, Bruce Springsteen's song "Glory Days" is actually about recalling and longing for the long-faded victories of youth. When I graduated, I was excited about the next phase of my life but had a vague fear that maybe high school was as good as it gets, and life would be all downhill from there. I couldn't have been more wrong! My high school years, awesome as they were, have paled in comparison to the last four years. God has made every one of my dreams come true, changing and using me more than I ever thought he could.

The teen years are an incredible, special, magical time of life, and we only get to live them once. But the fun, excitement and adventure are just beginning—there is so much to look forward to. College is an amazing experience and so, I am told, is marriage. (Give me four months, and I'll let you know for sure!) One of the things I love most about God is the way he never lets us become bored or stagnant in our lives—there are so many different stages to enjoy. I had always thought that once you got a job and got married, life settled down and stopped changing. Once I came to college, I experienced a revelation: Life is *always* changing, even in your adult years. High school graduation is just one of the first in a lifelong series of transitions.

If you are approaching this or any other milestone in your life, I urge you not to dwell on the past as the be-all and end-all of your life. Even if you do not know definite details about where you are headed after high school, as a disciple you can rest assured that the future holds great things for you. One thing you do know for sure: Your purpose of seeking and saving the lost will never change no matter what, nor will your relationship with God (except to grow better and stronger). If you remain faithful to him, he will give you a life that is more fulfilling and exciting than you can even imagine.

Will there be growing pains and adjustments to changes, and will there be difficulties along the way? Certainly! But you must decide this: No matter how difficult life may become at times, you will *never* back out of your vow to follow God. Even in the most challenging of life's circumstances, God is in absolute control, and he will bring about good from it in his own time. The Bible promises, "And we know that in *all* things God works for the good of those who love him" (Romans 8:28, emphasis added).

I believe that those of us who become Christians at a young age have a very special place in God's heart. You must understand that Satan is furious with you because you have escaped his clutches at such an early age. What a victory it would be for him if he manages to win back one of God's youngest followers. For this reason, he has concocted an awful but powerful plot to try to pull you away from God—if not during your teen years, then at some other point in your life. Decide now that you will see Satan's schemes for what they are and that you will never allow him to pull you away from God.

Let this warning give you a healthy fear of Satan's power, but don't become paranoid. By relying on God and his people you will not only survive the teen years, but soar through them triumphantly.

The more I see of the world, and the longer I am a part of the kingdom, the more I am convinced that we have the greatest lives of anyone on the planet. I am so thankful for my life that words fail me. I only know that with every passing year, my life has become even more wonderful, even more glorious. It is my prayer that your life too will exceed all of your greatest dreams. May you one day look back on the span of your life and realize with a smile of fulfillment that *all* of your days have been *glory days.*

DISCIPLESHIP PUBLICATIONS INTERNATIONAL

Who Are We?

Discipleship Publications International (DPI) began publishing in 1993. We are a nonprofit Christian publisher committed to publishing and distributing materials that honor God, lift up Jesus Christ and show how his message practically applies to all areas of life. We have a deep conviction that no one changes life like Jesus and that the implementation of his teaching will revolutionize any life, any marriage, any family and any singles household.

Since our beginning we have published more than 75 titles; plus we have produced a number of important, spiritual audio products. More than one million volumes have been printed, and our works have been translated into more than a dozen languages—international is not just a part of our name! Our books are shipped monthly to every inhabited continent.

To see a more detailed description of our works, find us on the World Wide Web at **www.dpibooks.com**. You can order books listed on the following pages by calling 1-888-DPI-BOOK twenty-four hours a day. From outside the US, call 781-937-3883, ext. 231 during Boston-area business hours.

We appreciate the hundreds of comments we have received from readers. We would love to hear from you. Here are other ways to get in touch:

> **Mail:** DPI, One Merrill St., Woburn, MA 01801
> **E-mail:** dpibooks@icoc.org

Find us on the
World Wide Web

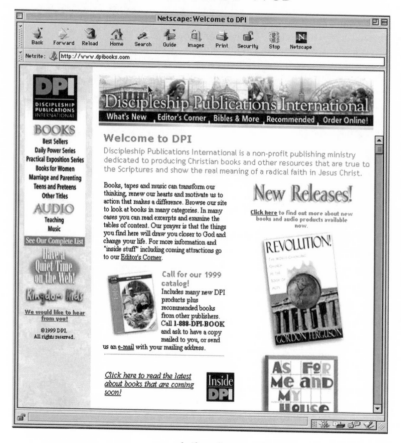

www.dpibooks.com
1-888-DPI-BOOK
outside US: 781-937-3883 x231

Take Hold of Life!

A Quiet Time Journal for Teens

When Paul wrote to his young friend and son in the faith, Timothy, he wanted more than anything for him to take hold! Not of sexual immorality. Not of a love of money. Not of false teachings. But to take hold of "faith and a good conscience." Of "deep truths." Of "eternal life." Of "life that is truly life." And God wants teens to take hold of the same things today. Each chapter contains the following:

- Devotional thought written by a teen
- Scriptures for further study
- "Food for Thought" questions
- "Extra" section to apply what you learn
- Thought for the Day
- Journal pages for responses
- Extra journal pages for sermon and class notes

Let It Shine

edited by Thomas & Sheila Jones

A quiet time book for teens. Straight talk about those fun but challenging teen years. Written by disciples who have spent a great deal of time working with teens and their needs. Includes a number of short readings by those who were teen disciples in the last few years.

The Killer Within

An African Look at Disease, Sin and Keeping Yourself Saved

by Mike Taliaferro

What do the Ebola virus, cholera, meningitis and the Guinea worm have to do with sin? In this poignant book you will find out. Mike Taliaferro has done it again! In his unique style he uses the physical world to paint a vivid picture of the deeper, more crucial issue of sin's effect on the soul. Powerful images of disease and sickness drive home the conviction that sin must never be taken lightly. But readers will go away full of hope understanding that while sin is serious, there is a Great Physician who heals and gives power over it.

The Lion Never Sleeps
by Mike Taliaferro

"Hooray for this book! A new sense of conviction is coming on God's people: We must keep the saved saved! Half of all those who are devoured by Satan, the 'roaring lion,' are less than six months old as Christians. Mike Taliaferro understands this problem. In *The Lion Never Sleeps*, he describes it in gripping detail, and then shows us God's solution. We must get back to the basics of making disciples—teaching them as we walk closely with them so they can fend off the attacks of Satan. This is not just a book of untried theories—Mike has put these principles into practice in the Johannesburg Church—and they work! *The Lion Never Sleeps* will result in keeping thousands of young disciples faithful who might otherwise be a meal for Satan. Read it, use it, recommend it to a friend."

—Al Baird, Elder, Los Angeles Church of Christ

ADVAITA

THE COMIC BOOK

IVÁN SENDE

NON-DUALITY PRESS

CHAPTER ONE

IT WAS NEW YEAR'S EVE AND LOTS OF PEOPLE WERE OUT.

ONE TICKET TO CHAIYA, PLEASE.

LUCKY YOU! IT'S THE LAST ONE LEFT FOR SURAT THANI.

I'VE NEVER BEEN A RELIGIOUS PERSON. IN FACT, ANYTHING SOUNDING REMOTELY SPIRITUAL WOULD INSTANTLY GIVE ME A RASH.

BUT AFTER MORE THAN A MONTH OF NON-STOP TRAVELING IN SOUTHEAST ASIA I DECIDED THAT IT WAS TIME TO TAKE A BREAK.

AND FOLLOWING THE EXAMPLE OF A FRIEND I MET ON MY TRAVELS, I DECIDED TO SIGN UP FOR A BUDDHIST MEDITATION RETREAT.

SUAN MOKKH?

SURE!

EXPERIENCING THAI CULTURE FIRST HAND APPEALED TO ME AND, TO BE QUITE HONEST, I WAS CURIOUS TO GET WHAT ALL THAT FUSS ABOUT BUDDHISM WAS.

SAWATI KRAP!

SAWATI KRAP!*

* "HELLO" IN THAI

IS THIS YOUR FIRST TIME HERE?

YES, AND YOU?

SIXTH.

WE GOT THERE EARLY, BUT THERE WERE ALREADY MANY PEOPLE WHO HAD ARRIVED THE DAY BEFORE.

KIWI!

GALICIA!

WHAT DO YOU KNOW ABOUT MEDITATION?

NOTHING.

GREAT!

IS THAT A GOOD ANSWER?

YES: THE BEST!

REALLY?

YES.

NEXT QUESTION...

AHEAD OF ME WERE TEN DAYS OF LEARNING HOW TO MEDITATE, IN SILENCE, GETTING UP AT FOUR IN THE MORNING, EATING TWO MEALS A DAY, AND SLEEPING ON A CONCRETE BED WITH A WOODEN PILLOW...

AT NIGHT THE GREAT SILENCE BEGAN.

DING!
DING!

* WALKING MEDITATION.

10

THE FIRST FEW DAYS IN THIS SORT OF RETREAT CAN BE HORRIBLE. IN FACT, MANY PEOPLE GIVE UP (ALMOST ALWAYS ON THE THIRD DAY) AND THE GROUP STARTS SHRINKING.

FIRST DAY

THE REASONS (EXCUSES?) FOR GIVING UP ARE VARIED: I DON'T GET IT, I DON'T SEE THE POINT IN IT, IT ISN'T WHAT I THOUGHT IT WOULD BE, IT HURTS MY BACK...

WHAT AM I DOING HERE WITH THIS HERD OF FREAKS?

SECOND DAY

AT A PHYSICAL LEVEL THE EXPERIENCE GOT TO BE GRUELING, WHICH ISN'T SURPRISING IF ONE TAKES INTO ACCOUNT THAT WE WERE SPENDING ABOUT EIGHT HOURS A DAY IN A POSITION WHICH WAS AWKWARD FOR A FARANG.

THIRD DAY

* THAI FOR "WESTERNER"

THE FACT THAT THE TEACHINGS WERE SO VERY REPETITIVE DIDN'T HELP EITHER.

BREATHE IN...

BREATHE OUT...

I WAS JUST ABOUT TO GIVE UP BECAUSE OF BACK PAIN.

I THINK I'M DOING SOMETHING WRONG.

CAN I SEE HOW YOU SIT?

LIKE THIS.

THAT WAY YOU WILL END UP HURTING YOU. YOU HAVE TO SIT UP STRAIGHT.

THAT'S IT!

BUT THIS WAY IS EVEN WORSE...

12

APART FROM THE PHYSICAL PROBLEMS AND INTERNAL STRUGGLES, MANY PEOPLE COULDN'T EMOTIONALLY ACCEPT CERTAIN BUDDHIST PRINCIPLES.

ACCORDING TO BUDDHA "YOU DO NOT EXIST."

TAN DHAMMAVIDU, AN ENGLISHMAN IN HIS SIXTIES, HAD BEEN LIVING AS A MONK FOR THE LAST FIFTEEN YEARS.

INDEPENDENT ENTITIES DO NOT EXIST. EVERYTHING IS IN A CONSTANT PROCESS OF BECOMING, THEREFORE: IN WHAT EXACT MOMENT DOES THE INDIVIDUAL APPEAR?

HE WAS THE ONE IN CHARGE OF EXPLAINING BUDDHA'S DOCTRINES.

THE ANSWER IS CLEAR: SUCH A THING DOES NOT EXIST, THE INDIVIDUAL DOES NOT EXIST.

HE ALWAYS HAD A PERSONAL ANECDOTE TO ILLUSTRATE THE DAILY TALKS.

I BELONG TO THE HIPPIE GENERATION.

YOU CAN ALL IMAGINE THE SORT OF THINGS I DID TO AMUSE MYSELF...

BUT EVEN WITH THE DISTRACTION OF HIS TALKS IT WASN'T EASY.

WHEN I WAS INTRODUCED TO BUDDHADASA BHIKKHU, THE FOUNDER OF THIS MONASTERY, THE FIRST THING I THOUGHT WAS: "AND SO THIS FAT GUY IS SUPPOSED TO BE ENLIGHTENED?"

I ALMOST GAVE UP, BUT I STUCK IT OUT. IF YOU'VE COME THIS FAR –I THOUGHT– YOU MUST REACH THE END.

I DECIDED TO STOP COMPLAINING ABOUT EVERYTHING, CALM DOWN, AND ACCEPT THE RULES OF THE GAME; I THINK IT WAS PROBABLY THIS CHANGE OF ATTITUDE WHICH CAUSED THINGS TO START WORKING.

IT TOOK ME THREE HORRIBLE DAYS TO ACCEPT THE CONDITIONS: TO SIT, RELAX, AND IGNORE EVERY THOUGHT THAT PASSES THROUGH YOUR MIND, BREATHE IN, BREATHE OUT...

16

I HAD TO ACCEPT, IN SPITE OF MY BASIC BELIEFS, THAT SOMEHOW THIS WORKED. OF COURSE THIS HAD SERIOUS IMPLICATIONS.

A DIFFERENT KIND OF KNOWLEDGE EXISTED, A REALITY THAT UP UNTIL THEN I HAD OVERLOOKED.

I HAD ALWAYS THOUGHT THAT THE MIND WAS WHAT UNDERSTOOD AND COMPREHENDED, THAT EVERYTHING WAS IN THE BRAIN – OUR TRUE TOOL FOR WORKING.

BUT THERE I FOUND OUT THAT THIS MIGHT NOT BE THE WHOLE TRUTH.

LUCKILY I'VE ALWAYS BEEN BLESSED WITH CURIOSITY. I ALWAYS WANTED TO UNDERSTAND WHY THINGS WERE AS THEY WERE, AND SO INSTEAD OF WORRYING ABOUT IT OR ADOPTING A DEFENSIVE ATTITUDE UPON SEEING HOW WHAT I HAD BELIEVED IN WAS QUESTIONED, I DELIGHTED IN THE POSSIBILITIES OPENING UP BEFORE ME.

IN FACT, I WAS EXCITED.

AND IF THIS MEDITATION THING WORKS —I THOUGHT— IF IT TURNED OUT THAT THESE WEREN'T FANTASIES OR PIOUS BELIEFS, THE NEXT QUESTION WAS SOON IN COMING.

WHERE DOES THIS ALL TAKE US?

WHAT IS THE MEANING, THE REAL PURPOSE OF THE BUDDHA'S TEACHINGS?

THE STORY OF THE BUDDHA
NAMO TASSA
BHAGAVATO ARAHATO
SAMMĀ-SAMBUDDHASSA
THE BUDDHA WAS BORN IN WHAT IS TODAY THE BORDER BETWEEN INDIA AND NEPAL, IN THE VILLAGE OF LUMBINI, WHEN HIS MOTHER, MAHAMAYA, WAS PASSING THROUGH ON A JOURNEY.
THE MOTHER DIED A FEW DAYS AFTER THE BIRTH AND THE BABY WAS BROUGHT BEFORE HIS FATHER, SUDDHODANA, KING OF THE SAKYAS. HE IN TURN BROUGHT THE BABY BEFORE THE WISE ASITA.
ASITA PREDICTED THAT THE BOY WOULD EITHER BE A GREAT WARRIOR OR A RELIGIOUS LEADER WITH MILLIONS OF FOLLOWERS. HE DECIDED TO CALL HIM SIDDHARTHA: HE WHO REACHES HIS GOAL.
THE FATHER WANTED THE BOY TO BECOME HIS SUCCESSOR TO THE THRONE. HE TRAINED HIM AS A WARRIOR AND NEVER ALLOWED HIM ACCESS TO THE OUTSIDE WORLD.
BUT PRINCE SIDDHARTHA WAS NOT HAPPY. HE MANAGED TO ESCAPE FROM THE PALACE THREE NIGHTS IN A ROW, AND THUS HE SAW HIS PEOPLE'S SUFFERING FIRST-HAND BY SEEING SICKNESS, OLD AGE, AND DEATH.

MOVED, HE DECIDED TO FLEE THE PALACE, ABAN-
DONING HIS PRINCE'S LIFE, AND RESOLVED TO SEEK A
SOLUTION TO SUFFERING.

FOR OVER FIVE YEARS HE PRACTICED AUSTERITIES
SEARCHING FOR THE ANSWER, REACHING THE
POINT OF DEATH ON NUMEROUS OCCASIONS.

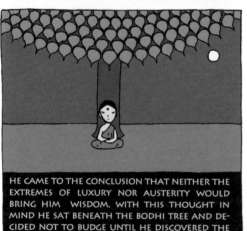

HE CAME TO THE CONCLUSION THAT NEITHER THE
EXTREMES OF LUXURY NOR AUSTERITY WOULD
BRING HIM WISDOM. WITH THIS THOUGHT IN
MIND HE SAT BENEATH THE BODHI TREE AND DE-
CIDED NOT TO BUDGE UNTIL HE DISCOVERED THE
DEFINITIVE ANSWER.

AFTER A FIERCE STRUGGLE WITH HIS INTERNAL
DEMONS, SIDDHARTHA ATTAINED ENLIGHTENMENT;
BEYOND SUFFERING, OLD AGE, AND DEATH, HE
REACHED THE EVERLASTING PEACE OF NIRVANA. THE
BUDDHA, THE AWAKENED ONE, WAS BORN.

AFTER SEVERAL DAYS OF PONDERING OVER WHAT
WOULD BE HIS NEXT MOVE, HE DECIDED TO DEDI-
CATE HIS LIFE TO SHARING WHAT HE HAD LEARNED.

HE SPENT THE REST OF HIS LIFE TRAVELLING,
SHARING HIS WISDOM WITH WHOEVER
WANTED TO LISTEN. HE DIED MANY YEARS LATER
SURROUNDED BY LOYAL FOLLOWERS.

I HAD ALWAYS TAKEN THAT STORY TO BE A MYTH, ONE WHICH WAS MORE OR LESS BEAUTIFUL, BUT A MYTH NONETHELESS.

WHILE STILL AT THE RETREAT I KEPT ON ASKING MYSELF "WHAT IS TRUE ABOUT ALL THIS?"

"WHAT DID BUDDHA MEAN WHEN HE CLAIMED TO HAVE FOUND THE END OF SUFFERING?

SUDDENLY THE WORD "ENLIGHTENMENT" TOOK ON NEW MEANING. WHICH ONE EXACTLY I COULDN'T SAY, BUT I WAS SURE THAT BEYOND SIMPLY MYTH OR LEGEND, IT MUST POSSESS A PROFOUND SIGNIFICANCE.

BASED ON MY OWN RECENT EXPERIENCE, THE IDEA SEEMED PLAUSIBLE.

I DECIDED THAT IT WAS WORTH INVESTIGATING.

COMPOSTELA, 2010

WITH TIME I STOPPED HASSLING MY FRIENDS WITH MY BUDDHISM KICK BUT I NEVER STOPPED RESEARCHING THE TOPIC, AND CONTINUED MEDITATING.

EVERY AFTERNOON I WOULD SIT FOR THIRTY MINUTES IN THE LIVING ROOM (I LIVED ALONE) AND CALMLY OBSERVE MY BREATHING.

THE TYPE OF MEDITATION I LEARNED AT THE RETREAT WAS ANAPANASATI, WHICH CONSISTED OF "16 SIMPLE STEPS TO ACHIEVING NIRVANA" AND IS PRACTICED MOSTLY IN THE THERAVADA BUDDHIST TRADITION.

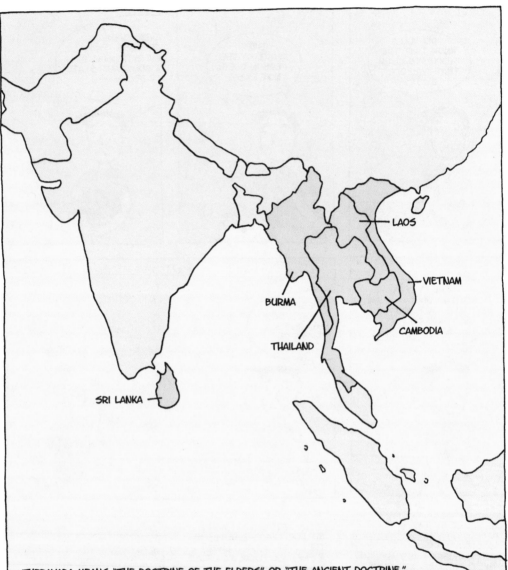

Map labels: LAOS, VIETNAM, BURMA, CAMBODIA, THAILAND, SRI LANKA

THERAVADA MEANS "THE DOCTRINE OF THE ELDERS" OR "THE ANCIENT DOCTRINE," THOUGH SOMETIMES ITS RIVALS INSIST UPON CALLING IT HINAYANA: "THE SMALL VEHICLE." IT IS THE OLDEST LIVING BRANCH OF BUDDHISM AND HAS PRACTICALLY DISAPPEARED IN INDIA, ITS HOMELAND. HOWEVER, THE TRADITION CONTINUES IN SRI LANKA AND IN SOUTHEAST ASIA, AND IS GAINING MOMENTUM IN THE WEST.

ITS DOCTRINAL CORPUS IS THE PALI CANON, WHICH IS THE FIRST GROUP OF BUDDHIST TEXTS WRITTEN BY THE COMMUNITY AFTER BUDDHA'S DEATH (400 YEARS LATER IN REALITY).

FOLLOWERS OF THERAVADA HAVE A VERY ORTHODOX VISION OF BUDDHISM AND BELIEVE, AMONG OTHER THINGS, THAT ENLIGHTENMENT CAN BE OBTAINED ONLY BY ONE WHO HAS BECOME A MONK OR LIVES RECLUSIVELY AND DEVOTED TO MEDITATION. AND EVEN WITH THIS BEING THE CASE, IT IS PROBABLE THAT THE PERSON MIGHT NEED SOME MERITS ACCUMULATED IN EARLIER LIVES TO BE WORTHY OF NIRVANA.

NOW YOU KNOW ONE OF THE REASONS WHY IT IS CALLED "THE SMALL VEHICLE": FEW PEOPLE ARE WILLING TO JUMP ON THIS WAGON.

KEEPING ALL THIS IN MIND IT MIGHT SEEM SLIGHTLY CRAZY TO EMBARK ON THIS TYPE OF ENTERPRISE, BUT:

ONE MUST UNDERSTAND THAT EVEN IF THE FINAL GOAL IS NOT REACHED, THE POSITIVE EFFECTS OF MEDITATION CAN BE BOTH FELT OVER TIME AND IN THE SHORT TERM.

IT'S TRUE. YOU WILL GAIN NOTHING BAD FROM THE MEDITATIVE PRACTICE. I LOOKED INTO THE MATTER DURING THOSE MONTHS; THE NEGATIVE CRITICISM CONSISTED IN LITTLE MORE THAN ANECDOTES WHILE THE BENEFITS, ON THE OTHER HAND, WERE NUMEROUS AND QUITE ATTRACTIVE:

–STRESS RELIEF
–IMPROVEMENT OF COGNITIVE CAPACITIES
–IMPROVEMENT IN MEMORY
–EMPOWERING OF EMOTIONAL INTELLIGENCE
–REDUCTION OF BLOOD PRESSURE
–STRENGTHENING OF THE IMMUNE SYSTEM
–IMPROVEMENT IN SELF-ESTEEM
–REINFORCEMENT OF EMPATHY

ETC...

AT ANY RATE, EACH AFTERNOON I WOULD SIT STILL AND QUIET, WILLING TO CLIMB THE STEPS OF THE ANAPANASATI LADDER.

IT WASN'T ALWAYS EASY. FROM TIME TO TIME I ARRIVED AT A STICKING POINT OR SUFFERED MOMENTS OF FEAR OR REJECTION, AND I DIDN'T KNOW HOW TO DEAL WITH THAT.

I BEGAN TO REALIZE THAT THE THERAVADA READINGS SPOKE A GREAT DEAL OF PHASES AND MEDITATIVE STATES BUT DIDN'T OFFER MUCH IN TERMS OF PRACTICAL ADVICE ON HOW TO HANDLE PRACTICAL PROBLEMS.

DESPITE THESE SMALL SETBACKS I CONTINUED TO INSIST WITH A PERSEVERANCE WHICH WAS UNUSUAL IN ME.

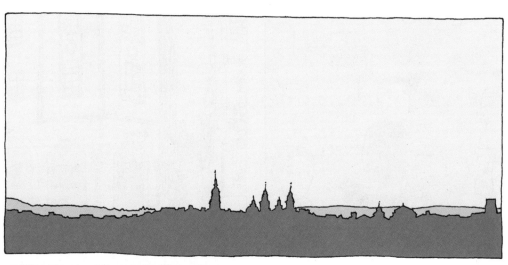

EACH SPRING, FOR MORE THAN A DECADE, MARKS THE BEGINNING OF MY WORK SEASON.

EVERY MORNING WITHOUT FAIL I WOULD GET UP AT AROUND TEN, EAT BREAKFAST, AND WALK TO "THE OFFICE."

I WASN'T AWARE OF IT AT THE TIME BUT I HAD ENTERED THE PHASE THAT CHRISTIAN MYSTICISM CALLS "THE PURGATIVE WAY".

REALLY TERRIBLE POSTURE

IN THE "PURGATIVE WAY" THE PERSON TURNS HIS OR HER BACK ON THE WORLD AND BEGINS TO LOOK INSIDE.

OLD HABITS AND PASTIMES TAKE A BACK SEAT.

IT MIGHT BE SAID THAT LIFE, AS IT HAS BEEN UNDERSTOOD UP TO THAT POINT, STARTS TO LOSE ITS APPEAL.

I WAS BEGINNING TO FOCUS ON WHAT IS CALLED "THE GREAT SEARCH."

IN BEING SO OBSESSED WITH A TOPIC, YOU'LL START SEEKING OUT THE COMPANY OF PEOPLE WITH SIMILAR LEANINGS, FOR EXAMPLE.

SO... YOU WENT ON A MEDITATION RETREAT?

YES...

YOU ALSO TRY TO INFORM YOURSELF AS BEST YOU CAN ON THE TOPIC.

CHECKING THESE OUT TODAY?

YES, PLEASE.

FINALLY, YOU EVEN END UP FINDING REFERENCES TO YOUR PASSION IN THE MOST UNEXPECTED PLACES.

THINGS CHANGE.

THEY ALWAYS DO.

IS ONE OF THE LAWS OF NATURE. MOST PEOPLE ARE AFRAID OF CHANGE, BUT IF YOU LOOK AT IT AS SOMETHING YOU CAN COUNT ON, THEN IT CAN BE A COMFORT.

IN MY CASE EVERYTHING THAT HAPPENED PASSED THROUGH –OR AT THE VERY LEAST BECAME RELATIVIZED BY– THE BUDDHIST SIFTER, THERAVADA IF POSSIBLE...

TIBETAN BOOK OF THE DEAD

THESE TIBETANS SURE ARE WEIRD!

IN ALL OTHER RESPECTS LIFE WENT ON AS USUAL.

YES, I MAKE THEM, THEY'RE ALL ORIGINAL WATERCOLORS.

ARE YOU TELLING ME THAT VEGETARIANS DON'T EAT TUNA EITHER?

34

I USUALLY TRAVEL DURING WINTER. THAT SUMMER I SPENT QUITE SOME TIME CHOOSING MY DESTINATION.

HOW DO YOU LIKE PATAGONIA IN WINTER?

...I MEAN IN SUMMER...

WELL... YOU KNOW WHAT I MEAN...

I'D SAY BUT ONE THING.

RUSSIA.

JAPAN IS THE BEST! BIT EXPENSIVE FOR YOU THOUGH...

IF I WERE YOU I'D GO TO THE STATES.

THERE'S NOTHING LIKE HOME.

FINALLY ENCOURAGED BY A COUPLE OF FRIENDS I CHOSE THE OPTION THAT SEEMED MORE NATURAL AFTER THE GOOD TIMES I HAD HAD IN SOUTHEAST ASIA.

IT WASN'T UNUSUAL THAT WHEN SOMEONE HEARD ABOUT THE TRIP, THEY STARTED IN WITH SPIRITUAL TALK.

OH! SO YOU'LL BE GOING TO INDIA AFTER ALL? IT MUST BE A VERY SPIRITUAL JOURNEY.

I EVEN GOT TO THE POINT OF POSITIONING MYSELF AGAINST ALL THAT. FINALLY I DECIDED THAT I WANTED TO GO, SEE FOR MYSELF, AND COME BACK SO THAT I COULD SAY THAT IT WAS NO BIG DEAL.

WHY DO YOU SAY THAT? I DON'T SEE WHY IT HAS TO BE LIKE THAT.

A SLIGHTLY ARROGANT ATTITUDE I'LL ADMIT.

DO YOU ALREADY KNOW WHERE YOU WANT TO VISIT?

I TRIED TO FOCUS ON THE TRIP'S CULTURAL ASPECTS, "ELEGANTLY" AVOIDING ANYTHING HAVING TO DO WITH HINDUISM.

GAGASTAN, I GUESS...

I HAD NO INTEREST IN LEARNING ANYTHING NEW OR DIFFERENT AT THE PHILOSOPHICAL OR SPIRITUAL LEVEL. I HAD ENOUGH ON MY PLATE WITH BUDDHISM TO EVEN THINK ABOUT OTHER TRADITIONS.

BUT HAD I REALLY APPLIED MY BUDDHIST KNOWLEDGE PERHAPS I WOULD HAVE ANTICIPATED THAT, AS THEY AFFIRM, EVERYTHING CHANGES; AND IN THIS CASE WHAT WAS GOING TO CHANGE WAS MY RELATIONSHIP WITH BUDDHISM ITSELF.

OR AS ANA, A FRIEND WHO WOULD ALSO BE GOING TO INDIA THAT SAME WINTER, SAID, IN REFERENCE TO ME:

IN THAILAND THEY'VE GIVEN HIM A TWIST, AND IN INDIA THEY'RE GONNA GIVE HIM THREE!

INDIA, WINTER 2010-11

I ARRIVED IN DELHI IN MID-NOVEMBER.

I HAD THREE MONTHS AHEAD OF ME TO DISCOVER THAT ENORMOUS COUNTRY.

SALAM-WALEICUM.

I THINK IT'S A GOOD IDEA TO GO TO INDIA WITH TIME TO SPARE, AND WITHOUT A DOUBT SPENDING A FEW DAYS GETTING USED TO IT IS RECOMMENDED.

NAMAST...

WALEICUMSALAM.

THE NON-STOP NOISE, THE STRONG SMELLS, THE CHARACTER OF THOSE PEOPLE, AT TURNS BRUTAL, CHILDLIKE, OR SIMPLY DISCONCERTING.

IN SHORT, IT'S A PLACE TO EASE INTO SLOWLY.

40

I SPENT THE FIRST FEW DAYS SIGHTSEEING, AND INTERESTING OPTIONS WERE NOT LACKING.

HARMANDIR SAHIB, AMRITSAR

MCLEOD GANJ

PUSHKAR

JODHPUR

41

BUT SOON I TOOK A BREAK FROM THE ROAD TO GO ON A BUDDHIST RETREAT.

AT THE OUTSET IT SEEMED SIMILAR TO THE ONE I HAD DONE IN THAILAND, ONLY THESE TYPES OF RETREATS WERE MUCH MORE POPULAR.

DID YOU WALK HERE?

YEAH, SOMEONE BROUGHT ME BY MOTORCYCLE UP TO THERE, AND THEN I CAME ON FOOT.

ANOTHER TEN DAYS IN SILENCE, IN THE DESERT, WITH ONLY A DOZEN COMPANIONS —A MIX OF INDIANS AND WESTERNERS— LISTENING TO RECORDINGS AND WATCHING VIDEOS ON THE SUBJECT.

THE MEDITATION SYSTEM WAS QUITE INTERESTING, HOWEVER THE TEACHING METHOD WAS LESS SO...

ANIIICCAAAAAAAAAAAAA

AFTER THE RETREAT I TRIED TO KEEP UP THE MEDITATION TECHNIQUE, BUT FOR WHATEVER REASON IT DIDN'T WORK.

SO... HOW WAS YOUR FIRST RETREAT?

REALLY GOOD!

GREAT!

WOULD YOU GUYS LIKE ME TO TAKE YOU TO JODHPUR?

OF COURSE!

IN FACT DURING THE REST OF MY STAY I TOOK A BREAK FROM MEDITATION.

DISCOVERING INDIA WAS KEEPING ME BUSY ENOUGH.

POP POP POP

AFTER LEAVING JODHPUR I HEADED SOUTH TO KARNATAKA, KERALA, TAMIL NADU...

LATER, ALREADY THINKING ABOUT THE RETURN HOME, I WENT UP NORTH AGAIN.
DESPITE HEARING A FEW NEGATIVE RECOMMENDATIONS, I COULDN'T RESIST
VISITING VARANASI.

THE LAST PLACE I HAD PLANNED TO VISIT WAS BODHGAYA, IN THE STATE OF BIHAR.

THIS LITTLE VILLAGE IS THE BUDDHIST PILGRIMAGE DESTINATION PAR EXCELLENCE FOR IT WAS THERE WHERE THE BUDDHA REACHED ENLIGHTENMENT SOME 25 CENTURIES AGO.

AFTER FINDING A ROOM (NOT AN EASY TASK, BY THE WAY) I MADE MY WAY TO THE TEMPLE WHERE THE BODHI TREE IS. IT IS A DESCENDENT OF THE FAMOUS ORIGINAL TREE AND IS LOCATED IN THE SAME SPOT –OR SO THEY SAY.

EVEN BY INDIAN STANDARDS IT WAS REALLY CROWDED.

I'D NEVER BEEN TO LOURDES, BUT THE FIRST THING I THOUGHT WAS THAT IT COULDN'T BE VERY DIFFERENT FROM THIS.

INSIDE THE TEMPLE THERE WHERE HUNDREDS OF PEOPLE TIRELESSLY PROSTRATING THEMSELVES. THE MAJORITY OF THEM DID THIS ON PLANKS WHICH HAD BEEN FASHIONED WITH THIS PURPOSE IN MIND.

ALTHOUGH THERE WERE ALSO SOME WHO WERE MORE MODEST AND WHO SIMPLY IMPROVISED CLOTH AND CARDBOARD PADDING AND KNEELED ON THE FLOOR.

THE TRUTH WAS THAT AT MOMENTS THE ATMOSPHERE RESEMBLED A GYM MORE THAN A PLACE OF WORSHIP.

AS FOR MYSELF, I DIDN'T QUITE GET THE CONNECTION BETWEEN ALL THIS AND THE BUDDHA'S TEACHINGS.

IF BUDDHA HAD SAID THAT THERE SHOULD BE NO ATTACHMENT TO ANYTHING: WHY DID THEY ADORE THAT PLACE, THAT TREE?

OF COURSE ON THE OTHER HAND I WAS ALSO THERE, CONTRIBUTING TO A CERTAIN EXTENT TO SUCH A CONTRADICTORY SITUATION.

THE LESS ATTRACTIVE FACET OF RELIGION —WHICH UP TO THAT POINT I HAD BEEN UNABLE TO SEE IN BUDDHISM— WAS AS PRESENT THERE AS IN ANY OTHER MAJOR RELIGIOUS CULT.

BUT I CAN'T SAY THAT BUDDHA, OR EVEN BUDDHISM, LET ME DOWN. THE SOLE RESPONSIBILITY FOR THIS DISENCHANTMENT RESTED ON ME.

BEFORE GETTING THE PLANE BACK IN DEHLI I DECIDED TO VISIT MY FRIEND ANA WHO WAS IN RISHIKESH.

LOCATED AT THE FOOT OF THE HIMALAYAS AND BLESSED WITH AN ENVIRONMENT CONDUCIVE TO RETREAT AND STUDY, RISHIKESH IS POPULARLY KNOWN AS THE "THE WORLD CAPITAL OF YOGA."

THE NAME RISHIKESH RINGS A BELL FOR MANY PEOPLE BECAUSE THE BEATLES WERE THERE BRIEFLY ON RETREAT. SPIRITUALLY IT DOESN'T APPEAR TO HAVE GONE TOO WELL FOR THEM, NEVERTHELESS IT WAS AN EXTREMELY PRODUCTIVE STAY: IT WAS THERE THAT THEY COMPOSED THE BULK OF WHAT BECAME THE WHITE ALBUM.

IN RISHIKESH THERE ARE LOTS OF COWS.

MONKEY GANGS.

AND SADHUS, ASCETICS WHO HAD ABANDONED ALL POSSESSIONS AND EARTHLY PRETENSIONS IN ORDER TO DEVOTE THEMSELVES EXCLUSIVELY TO THE SPIRITUAL QUEST.

THIS IS ALL IN THEORY, OF COURSE. THE REALITY IS THAT MANY OF THEM DEVOTE THEMSELVES TO BASICALLY DOING NOTHING OR GETTING HIGH ALL DAY.

AND OF COURSE THERE ARE ALSO YOGA STUDENTS. HERE "YOGA" IS UNDERSTOOD BROADLY. THE WORD YOGA LITERALLY MEANS "UNION" –IN THIS CASE THE UNION OF THE HUMAN WITH THE DIVINE– AND THEREFORE HERE YOGA WOULD BE ANY SORT OF ACTIVITY FOCUSED ON ATTAINING THIS UNION.

MANY OF THESE STUDENTS AND SOME TRAVELERS STAY IN ASHRAMS, WHICH ARE FAIRLY LARGE COMMUNITIES WHERE SILENCE AND TRANQUILITY REIGN.

BOY, IT IS IN FACT QUITE NICE HERE. IT'S A TRULY PLEASANT SPOT.

DOES THAT SURPRISE YOU? PEOPLE AREN'T DUMB. IF THEY COME HERE IT'S BECAUSE THEY KNOW THAT IT'S NICE.

AND HOW'S THE YOGA GOING?

PRETTY WELL. I'M GOING TO SEE A BRAZILIAN TEACHER. HE'S A BIT "PECULIAR," BUT HIS STYLE SUITS ME.

AND SINCE WE'RE ON THE TOPIC: WHAT DO YOU THINK ABOUT THIS WHOLE INDIAN SPIRITUALITY THING?

OH! IT'S GREAT!

I THINK IT'S A FASCINATING PLACE IN THAT SENSE.

SERIOUSLY?

YEAH, WHY? YOU DON'T?

WELL, IT'S LIKE WHAT SOMEONE I MET HERE TOLD ME: IF YOU FIND SPIRITUALITY IN INDIA IT'S BECAUSE YOU'VE ALREADY BROUGHT IT FROM HOME.

WELL I DON'T AGREE WITH THAT AT ALL. I FEEL THAT THERE ARE LOTS OF QUALIFIED PEOPLE HERE.

PARTICULARLY IN PLACES LIKE THIS ONE YOU CAN DISCOVER REALLY INTERESTING THINGS. OBVIOUSLY, THERE ARE SOME DOWNSIDES, THE SAME AS ANYWHERE ELSE, BUT STILL, I DON'T THINK THAT COMMENT IS VERY FAIR.

MAYBE YOU'RE RIGHT. I GUESS I'M JUST A LITTLE DISAPPOINTED.

TOMORROW THERE'S SATSANG HERE JUST AROUND THE CORNER. WOULD YOU LIKE TO COME?

SATSANG?

YES... A MEETING WITH A TEACHER, A GURU. YOU GO TO SEE HIM AND ASK HIM QUESTIONS, BUT ALL IN A VERY INFORMAL, RELAXED WAY.

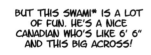

AND WHAT DO YOU THINK ABOUT THESE PEOPLE, THESE GURUS?

DO YOU THINK THEY'RE REALLY "ENLIGHTENED"?

WELL, THE TRUTH IS I DON'T KNOW WHAT TO THINK ABOUT THAT.

BUT THIS SWAMI* IS A LOT OF FUN. HE'S A NICE CANADIAN WHO'S LIKE 6' 6" AND THIS BIG ACROSS!

* HINDU EQUIVALENT OF "MONK"

THE NEXT DAY WE WENT TO SATSANG. THE SWAMI LOOKED AT US CALMLY AND CASUALLY ASKED US TO BRING UP ANY DOUBTS WE MIGHT HAVE.

HOW CAN ONE KNOW, WITH CERTAINTY, WHAT HIS OR HER GOAL IN LIFE IS?

BEING BORN HUMAN IS LIKE BEING GIVEN A FERRARI...

ARE YOU GOING TO LET IT RUST IN THE GARAGE?

OR ARE YOU GOING TO TAKE IT ON THE HIGHWAY AND SEE HOW FAST IT CAN GO?

I WASN'T THAT IMPRESSED BY THE THE MONK'S TALK, BUT ON THE OTHER HAND HE DIDN'T SEEM TO ME LIKE SOMEONE WHO WAS TRYING TO BE SOMETHING THAT HE WAS NOT. THERE WAS SOMETHING SINCERE, SOMETHING AUTHENTIC, IN HIM.

OM SHANTI SHANTI SHANTI.

BEFORE LEAVING RISHIKESH AND THE COUNTRY I VISITED A FEW BOOKSTORES, LOOKING FOR INTERESTING BOOKS RELATED TO THERAVADA. TO MY DISAPPOINTMENT THEY HAD VERY LITTLE ABOUT BUDDHISM, AND ALMOST NOTHING ON THERAVADA.

THERE'S SO MUCH TO CHOOSE FROM THAT IT'S HARD TO MAKE UP YOUR MIND, RIGHT?

YEAH!

SURE.

IN A PILE OF SECOND HAND BOOKS I SAW ONE THAT CAUGHT MY EYE. IT SEEMED TO BE IN EVERY INDIAN BOOKSTORE.

A FEW DAYS BEFORE IN DELHI...

WHAT'S THIS BOOK ABOUT?

OH, THAT BOOK...

THAT BOOK HAS CHANGED MANY PEOPLE'S LIVES...

THAT MIGHT BE THE CASE, BUT IT MIGHT NOT HAVE MUCH EFFECT ON ME.

BARGAINING (UNSUCCESSFULLY)

I READ A FEW SENTENCES FROM THE BOOK. THEY STRUCK ME AS BEING POWERFUL. AND SINCE IT WAS ON SALE (100 RUPEES CHEAPER THAN IN DELHI!) I BOUGHT IT, ALONG WITH A FEW OTHERS. FOR WHATEVER REASON I DIDN'T OPEN ANY OF THEM UNTIL A FEW MONTHS LATER.

AND SO, BETWEEN THIS AND THAT, IT WAS SOON TIME TO LEAVE.

CLAK

NOT WITHOUT SOME SADNESS, I MUST ADMIT.

HARI OM!

HARI OM!

INDIA LEAVES NO ONE INDIFFERENT. I DISCOVERED -WITH SOME SURPRISE- THAT I BELONGED TO THE GROUP OF THOSE WHO LOVE IT. WHEN IT CAME DOWN TO IT, I HAD TO ADMIT THAT IT WAS FASCINATING.

SOMETIMES IT IS DIFFICULT OR EVEN IMPOSSIBLE TO MEASURE
THE IMPACT THAT CERTAIN EVENTS CAN HAVE ON YOUR LIFE.
EVEN IN HINDSIGHT IT CAN BE IMPOSSIBLE TO EVALUATE THEM
FAIRLY.

LOOKING BACK, I THINK THAT THE MEETING WITH THE SWAMI AND
PURCHASING THAT BOOK, AND IN GENERAL MY ENTIRE STAY IN
INDIA, SEEMINGLY BANAL EVENTS, PLAYED A DECISIVE ROLE IN
EVERYTHING THAT WOULD FOLLOW.

IF SOMEONE HAD TOLD ME WHAT WAS GOING TO HAPPEN IN THE
COMING MONTHS, I'D PROBABLY THINK THAT THEY WERE JOKING.

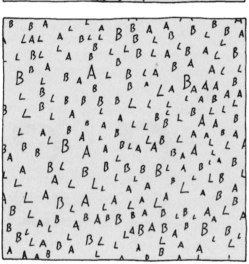

I ARRIVED IN PORTO IN MID-FEBRUARY. I WEIGHTED 10 POUNDS LESS AND MY BACKPACK, FULL OF BOOKS AND GIFTS, 10 POUNDS MORE.

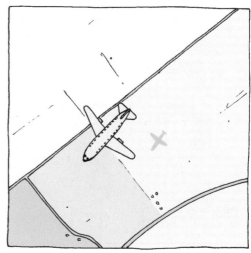

EACH TIME I RETURNED FROM MY TRAVELS I FOLLOWED THE SAME STRATEGY: I'D STAY WITH FRIENDS OR AT MY PARENTS' HOUSE FOR A WHILE, AND THEN I'D TAKE MY TIME IN FINDING A PLACE TO LIVE IN SANTIAGO, PREFERABLY NEAR "THE OFFICE."

HOWEVER, THAT YEAR A CHANGE WAS DUE.

I THINK WE NEED TO TALK.

CRAP!

DON'T YOU THINK WE SHOULD DO SOMETHING?

WHAT DO YOU MEAN?

I THINK THAT WE HAVE REACHED A PLATEAU.

AS THINGS STAND, WE'RE GOING NOWHERE. WE NEED SOME SORT OF CHANGE. IT'S ALL A BIT STRANGE: YOUR COMING AND GOING AND MY STAYING HERE, AS IF I WERE WAITING. AM I MAKING ANY SENSE?

SO WHY DON'T LIVE TOGETHER?

ARE YOU SURE?

WHY NOT?

THIS IS NUTS!

IF YOU DON'T HAVE MUCH MONEY, LOOKING FOR A FLAT IN COMPOSTELA CAN BE A DEPRESSING TASK. MANY OF THEM WOULD NEVER PASS A HEALTH INSPECTION.

HERE'S A SKETCH OF ONE OF THESE MARVELS. A BASEMENT TRANSFORMED INTO AN "APARTMENT."

KEEP IN MIND THAT A BED BARELY FITS IN THE BEDROOM.

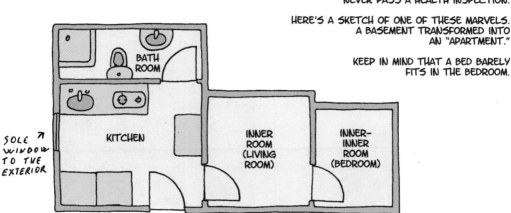

AFTER MANY VISITS AND MONEY SPENT ON PHONE CALLS WE CAME ACROSS A SMALL, BUT WELL-EQUIPPED, APARTMENT WHICH WAS NEAR TO WHERE I WORKED.

ALTHOUGH IT HAD NO HEATING, IT HAD BEEN RECENTLY REMODELED. OVER TIME, AND WITH A FEW PERSONAL TOUCHES, THE PLACE TURNED OUT TO BE QUITE COSY.

I STARTED DOING WATERCOLORS AND ANA VISITED WHENEVER SHE COULD.

I'LL MOVE IN LATER. RIGHT NOW I DON'T WANT TO LEAVE MY FATHER ALONE.

* AFTER "YO LA TENGO"

SPRING

I SPENT A LOT OF TIME EVERY DAY DEVOTED TO MY "SPIRITUAL STUDIES" BUT I ALWAYS TRIED TO MAKE THEM NOT TO INTERFERE WITH THE REST OF MY TASKS.

I'M HERE JUST ONE DAY A WEEK: DO YOU NEED TO DO YOUR MEDITATION NOW, REALLY?

I MAKE A DEAL WITH ANA THAT I WOULD SPEND ONE HOUR AT EVENING MEDITATING AND I WOULD KEEP ON SEARCHING INFORMATION ABOUT THAT ALL AT MY OWN EXPENSE.

YOU'RE RIGHT.

I'LL FIND TIME FOR MY STUFF WHEN YOU ARE AWAY.

ONE DAY I OPENED THE BOOK I HAD BOUGHT IN RISHIKESH —THE ONE THAT I SAW IN ALMOST VERY BOOKSHOP IN INDIA.

THE SENTENCES OF THAT MAN, NISARGADATTA, CAME TO ME LIKE BLOWS TO MY FACE.

WHO THE HECK IS THIS GUY?

I COULDN'T EVEN READ THE BOOK FOR LONG. I READ ONE OR TO SENTENCES AND THEN I PONDERED ABOUT THEM.

AND LITLLE BY LITTLE I INTRODUCED IN MY EVERYDAY MEDITATION THE TECHNIQUES THE AUTHOR DIRECTLY OR INDIRECTLY SUGGESTED.

WHO IS THE MEDITATOR?

WHO AM I ?

I HAD THE IMPRESSION THAT THE PROGRESS THAT I HADN'T MADE IN MONTHS OF BUDDHIST MEDITATION NOW TOOK PLACE SPONTANEOUSLY BY ASKING THOSE SIMPLE QUESTIONS.

I STARTED TO SEEK OUT INFORMATION ON THE ADVAITA VEDANTA TRADITION.

THAT'S HOW I DISCOVERED TEACHERS LIKE FRANCIS LUCILLE AND JEAN KLEIN.

Jean Klein - The Flame of Being

uttaraka · 5 videos

Subscribirse   65

14.046

Acerca de   Comparir   Engadir a

Gústame

FROM THE OUTSET I HAD THE IMPRESSION THAT THEY WERE DIFFERENT FROM THE OTHER TEACHERS (MAINLY BUDDHISTS) THAT I'D KNOWN UP UNTIL THEN.

LIFE, CONSCIOUSNESS... WE CANNOT OBJECTIFY IT.

AND THEY WERE DIFFERENT FOR A VERY SIMPLE REASON: THEIR WORDS DIDN'T APPEAR TO DEPEND ON A PHILOSOPHY, A RELIGION, OR A SYSTEM OF BELIEFS. THEY SPOKE OF ULTIMATE REALITY, BUT FROM EXPERIENCE.

CONSCIOUSNESS IS THE ULTIMATE SUBJECT.

THERE WERE SOME TEACHERS OF THAT ADVAITA VEDANTA WHO INSPIRED TRUST IN ME. HOWEVER, THE IMPLICATIONS OF THE THINGS THEY SAID STRUCK ME AS TOO PROVOCATIVE.

OF COURSE THIS WASN'T SURPRISING CONSIDERING WHERE I CAME FROM.

The Flower of Dhamma
999 likes · 156 talking about this

🖒 **Like** | ⚙ ▼

Non-Profit Organization
Practice & Studies on Theravada Buddhism

👍 **999**

About

Likes

Photos | Events | Twitter

 The Flower of Dhamma created an event.
June 22 🌐

 DEBATE: AWAKENING IN THE 21ST CENTURY
Do you think it's possible to reach englightenment during these times of crisis?

3 talking about this

Like · Comment · Follow Post · Share

Henar S. well i'm not sure, but there's no doubt that the beginning of this century is challenging for buddhist patience!
June 23 at 2:16 am via mobile · 🖒 1

Like · Comment · Follow Post · Share

Paulo Otero I would settle for being able to concentrate on my breathing for five minutes ;)
June 23 at 2:46 pm via mobile · 🖒 2

Like · Comment · Follow Post · Share

Lieutenant Maro lately i've been pretty busy. it looks like i'll leave it for my next reincarnation XD
June 22 at 3:14 am via mobile · 🖒 1

Likes | See All

Compostela Buddhist Association
Church/Religious Organization

🖒 Like

Zen-ith
Community

🖒 Like

📋 **Activity**
Recent

The Flower of Dhamma created **VIPASSANA MEDITATION**

THE MAJORITY OF BUDDHIST TRADITIONS INSIST ON THE FACT THAT THE BUDDHA WAS JUST ANOTHER MAN, NOT A GOD OR A SUPERMAN, BUT RATHER A PERSON OF FLESH AND BLOOD, AND THAT JUST AS HE WAS ABLE TO REACH NIRVANA, SO TOO CAN ANYONE ELSE (AFTER ALL, THIS IS THE GOAL OF THE BUDDHIST PRACTICE). HOWEVER, IT SOON BECOMES CLEAR THAT THE VAST MAJORITY OF THEM CONSIDER THIS NIRVANA TO BE BEYOND THEIR REACH, SOMETHING RESERVED FOR UNDOUBTEDLY EXTRAORDINARY PEOPLE.

I HAD ASSIMILATED THIS PERSPECTIVE WITHOUT EVEN REALIZING IT, UP TO THE POINT THAT EVERYTHING SURROUNDING HINDUISIM SEEMED FRIVOLOUS TO ME BECAUSE IT TREATED THE IDEA OF AWAKENING -ENLIGHTENMENT- AS SOMETHING REALLY ACCESSIBLE, SOMETHING NATURAL AND ACHIVABLE...

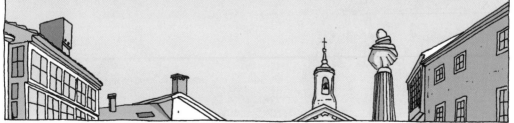

VEDANTA IS ONE OF THE SIX GREAT PERSPECTIVES OF INDIAN KNOWLEDGE, AND ADVAITA IS THE NAME OF ITS MOST WELL-KNOWN AND INFLUENTIAL BRANCH.

ADVAITA LITERALLY MEANS "NOT-TWO," A NAME WHICH REFERS TO THE ULTIMATE REALITY. LIKE OTHER NON-DUAL TRADITIONS SUCH AS TAOISM OR SUFISM, THE ADVAITA VEDANTA CONTINUALLY POINTS TO THE INEFFABLE UNITY OF ALL THINGS: ALL IS ONE.

FOR THE PRACTITIONER OF VEDANTA THE MAIN PROBLEM, THE CAUSE OF SUFFERING, IS IGNORANCE, A LACK OF AWARENESS, OF WHO WE REALLY ARE. THE GOAL OF THE STUDENT, THEREFORE, IS TO OVERCOME THIS IGNORANCE AND BE ABLE TO RECOGNIZE THE TRUE NATURE OF THE SELF. HOWEVER THIS RECOGNITION ISN'T WORTH MUCH IF IT IS MERELY INTELLECTUAL; ACCORDING TO THE VEDANTA TRADITION, VALID KNOWLEDGE MUST BE ANCHORED IN EXPERIENCE.

I CONTINUED TO DEEPEN MY KNOWLEDGE IN THE TEACHINGS AND FROM TIME TO TIME SAW SOME VIDEOS ON THE INTERNET ABOUT CONTEMPORARY TEACHERS OR READ BOOKS BY CLASSIC AUTHORS LIKE RAMANA MAHARSHI.

SOON MY MEDITATION SHIFTED NATURALLY FROM THE GRADUAL AND PROGRESSIVE SYSTEM OF THERAVADA BUDDHISM TO THE SIMPLER AND MORE DIRECT METHOD THAT THESE OTHER TEACHERS PROPOSED, UNTIL FINALLY LEAVING THE FORMER BEHIND. IT FELT MUCH MORE COMFORTABLE THIS WAY, AND OVER TIME I REALIZED THAT, WITH ITS UPS AN DOWNS, MY MEDITATION HAD SHIFTED DIRECTION AND WAS, TO A CERTAIN EXTENT, DEEPER AND MORE INTENSE, AND HAD EVEN BEGUN TO FIND ITS WAY NATURALLY INTO DAILY LIFE.

AND WHILE I ENGAGED IN THE SPIRITUAL SEARCH, THE WORLD HEADED STRAIGHT FOR ECONOMIC CRISIS.

WHAT WOULD I HAVE TO DO TO WORK ON THIS STREET WITH YOU GUYS?

DURING THOSE MONTHS IT WENT FROM BEING JUST A TOPIC OF CONVERSATION TO A MORE AND MORE PALPABLE REALITY.

HOW MUCH DOES THAT PERMIT COST?

THERE WAS ALWAYS SOMEONE ASKING ABOUT HOW THEY COULD JOIN OUR CLUB. BUT THAT YEAR WAS IMPRESSIVE.

WHAT IF I WERE TO JUST SET UP HERE, TUCKED AWAY IN A CORNER?

THINGS STARTED TO SLOW DOWN FOR US TOO.

CAN YOU BELIEVE THAT IT'S LUNCHTIME AND I HAVEN'T SOLD A THING?

THIS IS THE END, FOLKS...

IT'S THE APOCALYPSE!*

* PEOPLE WORKING IN THE STREET ARE USUALLY A BIT DRAMATIC

♪ESTAS SON LAS MAÑANITAS ...

ESTAS SO

BLOWN-OUT LOUDSPEAKER HIDDEN IN BACKPACK

73

MOREOVER, I HAD OTHER IMPORTANT THINGS TO DEAL WITH.

I THINK WE SHOULD TALK ABOUT YOUR PROBLEM.

PROBLEM?

WHAT PROBLEM?

I HAVE NEEDS.

NEEDS?

SEE!

YOU DON'T EVEN REALIZE IT!

I HAVE AFFECTIVE NEEDS, SEXUAL NEEDS!

IT'S BEEN OVER A WEEK SINCE WE LAST DID IT...

ARE YOU SURE?

A WEEK?

ONE SIDE-EFFECT OF THE PURGATIVE WAY IS THAT THE WORLD AND ITS CONCERNS CEASE TO BE OF ANY INTEREST.

MORE THAN A WEEK.

THIS SURELY WAS MY CASE.

I THINK YOU SHOULD MAKE AN EFFORT.

I'LL TRY. BUT IF I'M NOT FEELIN' IT, WHAT CAN I DO?

I LOST INTEREST IN WORK, IN MY RELATIONSHIP, IN MY FRIENDS, MY HOBBIES...

YOU CAN'T FORCE THIS SORT OF THING.

BY THAT TIME I WAS REALLY INTO THAT SEARCH THING. LOOKING AT MY "SPIRITUAL HEROES", I CONSIDERED THAT I WAS BEING QUITE SENSIBLE.

BUDDHA: SIX YEARS OF MORTIFICATIONS.

MAHAVIRA: THE FOUNDER OF JAINISM SPENT OVER TWELVE YEARS NAKED PRACTICING EVERY KIND OF AUSTERITIES ACCEPTING WITH EQUANIMITY WHATEVER MIGHT HAPPEN TO HIM.

BODHIDHARMA: ACCORDING TO THE MOST POPULAR ACCOUNTS OF HIS LIFE THE BUDDHIST PATRIARCH SPENT 9 YEARS OF HIS LIFE STARING AT A WALL.

SUMMER

AS THE YEAR WENT ON MY SEARCH BECAME MORE INTENSE, AND LITTLE BY LITTLE I STARTED TO PUT EVERYTHING THAT HAD HAPPENED TO ME INTO PERSPECTIVE. READINGS SUCH AS THE "TALKS WITH RAMANA MAHARSHI", WHICH AT FIRST SEEMED CONFUSING TO ME, STARTED TO BECOME ACCESSIBLE.

DURING MEDITATION I BEGAN TO SUCCESSFULLY FACE EMOTIONS SUCH AS FEAR.

IN GENERAL I BEGAN TO CARRY MY RESEARCH INTO MY EVERYDAY LIFE.

I TOOK ADVANTAGE OF ANY PLACE OR SITUATION TO INVESTIGATE.

RESIDENTS OF THE OS MAIOS NEIGHORHOOD OF A CORUNA ARE PROTESTING AGAINST THE HEAVY CONSTRUCTION TAKING PLACE THERE THESE DAYS. THE CITY BUS HAS BEEN UNABLE TO CARRY OUT TWO OF ITS ROUTINE STOPS.

I THINK IT'S DEPLORABLE. THERE ARE PEOPLE HERE THAT HAVE TO WALK ALMOST A QUARTER OF A MILE FROM THEIR HOUSE TO THE BUS STOP. IT'S NOT FAIR!

OBSERVATION, MINDFULNESS —WHICH PROPERLY UNDERSTOOD IS NOTHING BUT MEDITATION— TOOK UP ALL OF MY TIME.

WELL, AT LEAST THEY'LL GET SOME EXERCISE.

I OBSERVED MY THOUGHTS, MY WORDS, AND MY REACTIONS CONSTANTLY, 24 HOURS A DAY.

THEY'RE ALWAYS COMPLAINING ABOUT SOMETHING.

WHEN I FALTERED THERE WAS ALWAYS SOMEONE TO REMIND ME.

MAYBE THERE ARE ELDERLY PEOPLE OR SOME OF THEM HAVE TROUBLE WALKING. ANYWAY, NOT EVERYONE LIKES WALKING, LIKE YOU.

SHE'S RIGHT. WHY DID I SAY THAT? I SAID IT WITHOUT EVEN THINKING.

IN FACT, IT WAS STRANGE. AT SOME POINT, EACH TIME I LOST THIS ATTENTION AND MADE A JUDGMENT, EACH TIME I CRITICIZED SOMEONE ELSE, THE BALL BOUNCED BACK TO ME.

IT NEVER FAILED.

THAT'LL BE FOURTEEN FORTY-SIX.

ONE,

TWO,

AND...

OH MY!

I'M NOT SURE I BROUGHT ENOUGH MONEY.

COME ON LADY! I'M IN A HURRY, AND NOW THIS!

IT'S LIKE SOMEBODY WAS ASKING, "WHO ARE YOU TO JUDGE?"

THAT'LL BE EIGHT SIXTY, PLEASE.

NOTHING VERY SPECTACULAR, BUT IT WAS AN EFFECTIVE WAY TO RETURN ME TO ATTENTIVENESS.

UH, WELL... IT LOOKS LIKE I LEFT MY MONEY AT HOME.

FUNNY, AIN'T IT?

IN THE FORMAL MEDITATION SESSIONS I BEGAN TO INCORPORATE MY OWN TECHNIQUES (EVEN THOUGH I LATER FOUND OUT THAT THESE WERE DONE BY MANY OTHERS).

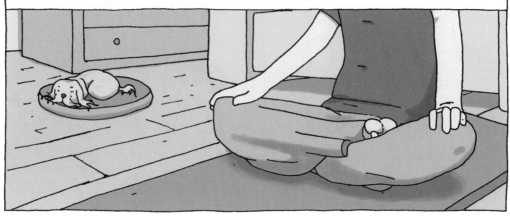

WHAT IS THAT THAT NEVER SLEEPS?

SHORTLY AFTER ASKING MYSELF THIS QUESTION, "WHO OR WHAT IS THAT THAT NEVER SLEEPS?" I FOUND THAT I BEGAN TO EXPERIENCE ODD CHANGES IN MY SLEEP. DURING ALMOST AN ENTIRE WEEK I HAD SOMETHING LIKE A CONSCIOUS SLEEP: I SLEPT, BUT SOMEHOW REMAINED CONSCIOUS.

I ASKED AN ADVAITA TEACHER ABOUT THIS VIA HIS WEB PAGE. ASIDE FROM HIS RESPONSE, WHICH WAS ALMOST INSTANTANEOUS, I GOT SURPRISED BY THE FACT THAT A PERSON WHO I HELD IN HIGH ESTEEM IN THIS WORLD —THE SPIRITUAL ONE— TOOK MY QUESTION SO SERIOUSLY.

I HAD ASKED THE QUESTION WITH SOME HESITATION, BUT HE RESPONDED CLEARLY AND CONCISELY, ASSUMING THAT WHAT I WAS TELLING HIM WAS INSCRIBED WITHIN THE FRAMEWORK OF A MATURE QUEST. THIS GAVE THE WHOLE PROCESS A POWERFUL PUSH FORWARD.

SOMETIMES I MADE USE OF "THE WITNESS TECHNIQUE."

MOST OF US IDENTIFY OURSELVES WITH OUR THOUGHTS, SOMETHING THAT QUICKLY BECOMES QUESTIONED AS SOON YOU START PRACTICING ANY OF THE MOST COMMON MEDITATION TECHNIQUES. SOON YOU CAN SEE HOW YOUR THOUGHTS PASS BEFORE YOU LIKE CLOUDS DRIFTING ACROSS THE SKY. IN ADDITION TO IDENTIFYING OURSELVES WITH OUR THOUGHTS, WE ALSO ASSOCIATE OUR BEING –THAT WICH WE CALL "I"– TO A SERIES OF SENSATIONS, EVEN PHYSICAL ONES. SOMEHOW WE HAVE THIS FEELING THAT WE LIVE SOMEWHERE INSIDE THE CHEST OR, MORE COMMONLY, INSIDE THE HEAD. BUT IS THIS TRUE? ARE WE SOME SORT OF DIFFUSE ENTITY RESIDING BETWEEN THE EARS?

THE THEORY OF THE WITNESS TECHNIQUE IS SIMPLE: IF YOU CAN SEE A FLOWER THIS MEANS THAT YOU ARE NOT THE FLOWER. IF YOU CAN SEE A THOUGHT, THIS MEANS THAT YOU ARE NOT THAT THOUGHT. WHEN YOU LOCATE YOURSELF AS THE WITNESS, YOU PUT EVERYTHING –THOUGHTS, FEELINGS, AND PERCEPTIONS– AT THE SAME LEVEL.

IT'S AS IF YOU WERE STANDING SOMEWHERE SIX INCHES BEHIND YOUR OWN HEAD AND FROM THAT VANTAGE POINT YOU OBSERVE EVERYTHING THAT HAPPENS WITHOUT IDENTIFYING YOURSELF WITH ANYTHING. THEREFORE, THE PLANT THAT YOU ARE WATERING AND THE LAST THOUGHT THAT HAS PASSED THROUGH YOUR MIND ARE ON THE SAME LEVEL: NEITHER OF THEM ARE YOU, YOU ARE THE WITNESS, THE IMPARTIAL OBSERVER OF IT ALL.

AT FIRST IT WAS DIFFICULT TO PUT MYSELF IN THIS SITUATION, BUT IN TIME IT TURNED OUT TO BE EVEN FUNNY.

AT ANY RATE THE TRULY INTERESTING PART OF ALL OF THESE TECHNIQUES AND EXERCISES IS THAT THEY WERE A TREMENDOUS HELP IN TERMS OF QUESTIONING THE IDEAS AND PRECONCEPTIONS THAT I ALWAYS HAD REGARDING MY OWN IDENTITY. THEY CAUSED ME TO REPEATEDLY RETURN TO THE FUNDAMENTAL QUESTION:

WHO AM I?

IN THE WORLD, ASIDE FROM THE CRISIS, THERE WAS OTHER NEWS, SOME BEING CAUSED BY THE CRISIS ITSELF.

SOMEONE SPOKE BEFORE ABOUT EARLY CHILDHOOD EDUCATION...

THAT WAS THE YEAR OF 15-M AND REAL DEMOCRACY NOW! THE MAJORITY OF US STARTED LEARNING ABOUT WHAT IT WAS ALL ABOUT WHEN IT WAS ALREADY WELL UNDERWAY.

I THINK THAT CURRENTLY EDUCATION IS FOCUSED ON STIFLING CREATIVITY

PEOPLE BROUGHT FOOD TO THESE MAKESHIFT CAMPSITES. DURING THE DAY DIFFERENT PROPOSALS WERE WORKED ON AND DISCUSSED AND EACH AFTERNOON THERE WAS AN ASSEMBLY THAT ANYONE COULD PARTICIPATE IN.

ON PUTTING UP BARRIERS, ON TEACHING YOU HOW THE WORLD IS.

AFTER WORK I DROPPED BY THE ASSEMBLIES THAT MET IN OBRADOIRO SQUARE EACH DAY AT AROUND EIGHT.

NOT ON LETTING YOU LEARN FOR YOURSELF...

THE TALKS THAT I MOST APPRECIATED CAME FROM THE YOUNGEST PEOPLE.

...TO CULTIVATE THAT WORLD THAT YOU CARRY INSIDE.

EVEN THOUGH THE MOVEMENT HAD ITS OCCASIONAL DARK FACETS, I THINK THAT IN GENERAL IT WAS A BREATH OF FRESH AIR FOR A SOCIETY THAT HAD BEEN ASLEEP.

I THINK THAT IN THIS SENSE THE OLDER WE GET THE MORE WE UNLEARN.

I BELIEVE THAT IT BROUGHT TO MANY PEOPLE THE NOTION THAT CHANGE, BASED ON A MODEL WHICH WAS FAIRER AND MORE PARTICIPATIVE, WAS REALLY POSSIBLE.

I'D LIKE ONE OF OUR GOALS HERE TO BE THE CREATION OF AN EDUCATIONAL SYSTEM THAT DOESN'T COME AND GO WITH THE DIFFERENT GOVERNMENTS IN OFFICE, BUT RATHER ONE THAT BECOMES PROGRESSIVELY MORE ENRICHED, ADAPTING ITSELF TO THE CHANGING TIMES.

HOWEVER, AT A CERTAIN POINT I HAD TO CHOOSE WHETHER TO FOLLOW THE SHIFTS OF THOSE PEOPLE OR FOCUS ON MY OWN CRUSADE.

I FELT THAT GOING TO THE ASSEMBLIES DISTRACTED ME, GOT ME INVOLVED IN THE DEBATES, AND THAT I LOST THE INTROSPECTIVE MOOD THAT I HAD BEEN CULTIVATING ALL SUMMER.

AND THIS IS JUST A SMALL SAMPLE OF ALL THE THINGS I LEFT BEHIND DURING THOSE DAYS. ACTUALLY I THINK I NEVER WAS COMPLETELY AWARE OF HOW FAR MY COMMITMENT WITH ALL THAT SPIRITUAL THING HAD GONE.

BECAUSE THAT'S THE TRUE SOLUTION TO PROBLEMS: CREATIVITY.

CLAP!
CLAP!
CLAP!

THANK YOU!

TOWARDS THE END OF THAT SUMMER MY DRIVE TO FIND THE TRUTH –TRUTH WITH A CAPITAL T– DISPLACED ALL OTHER INTERESTS. NEVERTHELESS, I WAS AWARE OF THE FACT THAT I ALREADY HAD TRIED EVERYTHING, AND AS HARD AS POSSIBLE... IN VAIN.

ON THE ONE HAND THIS QUEST HAD COME TO SIGNIFY MY ONE AND ONLY INTEREST, AND ON THE OTHER I DIDN'T HAVE A CLUE HOW TO GO ABOUT IT.

I WAS LOST.

I THOUGHT THAT IF ACHIEVING THAT –ENLIGHTENMENT, AWAKENING– WAS POSSIBLE, IT SHOULD BE POSSIBLE TO DO IT ON YOUR OWN, BUT IT GOT TO THE POINT WHERE I FELT POWERLESS. I DECIDED THAT I NEEDED HELP, I NEEDED A GUIDE, A REFERENCE POINT. AND WHERE COULD I FIND A TEACHER IN THE ADVAITA TRADITION? THE ANSWER WAS OBVIOUS: INDIA, THE CRADLE OF VEDANTA.

THE DECISION TO RETURN TO INDIA IN ORDER TO SEEK OUT A TEACHER WAS VERY MEANINGFUL: IT MEANT THAT I WAS WILLING TO DO ANYTHING IN ORDER TO REACH MY OBJECTIVE, WHETHER IT WAS FINDING A GURU, BECOMING A MONK, RENOUNCING EVERYTHING I HAD, OR RISK FALLING INTO A SECT: I DIDN'T CARE.

I HAD AN INCREDIBLE FAMILY, CHARMING FRIENDS, I LOVED ANA, AND I DID APPRECIATE MY JOB, BUT AT A CERTAIN POINT ALL THIS BECOMES SECONDARY: LIFE ITSELF IS THROWN INTO DOUBT, AND THE SEEKER PREFERS TO GIVE HIS LIFE RATHER THAN LIVE IN IGNORANCE. AT A CERTAIN POINT YOU WOULD DIE FOR THE TRUTH, AND NOT IN TERMS OF METAPHOR, BUT IN A VERY REAL SENSE.

WITH REGARD TO THE SITUATION WITH ANA, I WAS TO A CERTAIN DEGREE AWARE OF WHAT WAS HAPPENING.

YOU'RE NOT GOING TO SAY ANYTHING?

BUT IT SEEMED SECONDARY TO ME.

ANYTHING ABOUT WHAT?

IT WAS AS IF THE EVENTS OF DAILY LIFE HAD BECOME RELEGATED TO MERELY A BACKGROUND NOISE.

SOMETHING, I DON'T KNOW, ANYTHING.

IT STRIKES ME AS SAD —THE TWO OF US, HERE, WITH NOTHING TO SAY.

WELL, I DON'T HAVE ANYTHING TO SAY. TO BE HONEST, I THOUGHT THAT WE WERE BOTH SIMPLY HERE EATING BREAKFAST PEACEFULLY.

FORGET IT...

I LIKE IT, BUT I THINK YOU SHOULD GET A SECOND OPINION.

FURTHER ALONG, BY NOW I THINK IT'S GOING WELL. AND BESIDES, I TRUST YOUR STANDARDS.

YOU'RE STILL NOT CLEAR ON IT, HUH?

IT'S JUST THAT YOU'RE INVESTING A LOT OF YOURSELF IN THIS, AND YOU MIGHT BE DISAPPOINTED.

I LIKE IT, BUT I KNOW THAT IN PART IT'S BECAUSE IT'S CONNECTED WITH ME. I DON'T KNOW WHAT I WOULD THINK ABOUT IT IF IT HAD NOTHING TO DO WITH ME. THE SPIRITUAL THEME ISN'T A POPULAR ONE, NOT TO MENTION IN COMIC FORMAT...

YOU KEEP THINKING THAT IT'S SOMETHING MADE FOR A SPIRITUAL AUDIENCE, BUT THIS ISN'T THE CASE HERE. IT'S A COMIC MADE FOR PEOPLE WHO LIKE COMICS, PEOPLE WHO LIKE ALL KINDS OF STORIES.

THANKS.

IN THE SAME WAY THAT OTHER COMICS DISCUSS SICKNESS, SEXUALITY, OR EVEN WAR, THIS ONE DEALS WITH THE THE SPIRITUAL QUEST. THE SUBJECT IS LESS IMPORTANT THAN THE WAY YOU TREAT IT.

-CHUP-

OK, OK, BUT IT'S NOT THE SAME. THOSE ARE IMPORTANT QUESTIONS OR ONES OF SOCIAL INTEREST. THE SPIRITUAL ISSUE ISN'T SOMETHING THAT AFFECTS THAT MANY PEOPLE.

I DON'T AGREE. EVERYONE HAS SPIRITUAL INTEREST, EVEN IF THEY DON'T CHOOSE TO CALL IT LIKE THAT. YOU MIGHT SAY THAT THE SPIRITUAL QUEST IS SIMPLY THE SEARCH FOR HAPPINESS, AND WE'RE ALL LOOKING FOR HAPPINESS: WE ALL WANT TO BE TRANQUIL AND AT PEACE WITH OURSELVES.

FEELING GOOD, FEELING HAPPY IS A SPIRITUAL EXPERIENCE OF THE HIGHEST DEGREE EVEN THOUGH THE MAJORITY OF PEOPLE WOULD NEVER THINK OF CALLING IT THIS WAY. "SPIRITUAL" IS A NAME, A LABEL: FORGET ABOUT ALL THAT. FACTS ARE WHAT COUNT.

YOU SHOULD GET A SECOND OPINION.

89

AUTUMN

I STOPPED WORKING IN MID-OCTOBER.

ANA, HOWEVER, WAS INAUGURATING A PRINTMAKING EXHIBITION IN EARLY NOVEMBER IN A SMALL TOWN IN THE PROVINCE OF OURENSE.

WHICH DO YOU THINK IS BETTER?

THAT ONE!

ARE YOU SURE?

BETWEEN THE STRESS FROM THE INAUGURATION AND HER WORRIES ABOUT HER FATHER, WHO WAS GETTING OLD AND LIVED ALONE, ANA BEGAN TO HAVE IRREGULAR HEART RHYTHMS AND ANXIETY ATTACKS.

I THINK MY HEART IS GOING TO STOP.

RELAX, IT'LL PASS.

IN THE SPIRITUAL SEARCH THERE ARE MOMENTS OF BLISS AND OTHERS OF DARKNESS. JUST PRIOR TO GOING TO OURENSE I EXPERIENCED TWO DAYS OF UTTER HAPPINESS: CLEAR, PURE, CAUSELESS JOY.

BUT IT PASSED, IT TOO PASSED, AND THE SLIP BACK INTO DOUBT AND CONFUSION WAS PAINFUL AND DISCONCERTING.

I DID THE BEST I COULD. I FORGOT ABOUT IT AND FOCUSED ON HELPING ANA.

HOW IS IT LIKE THIS?

BETTER.

AND ALTHOUGH THE WORD RESIGNATION COMES TO MIND, IN REALITY IT WASN'T THIS. IT WOULD BE FAIRER TO CALL IT ACCEPTANCE: I HAD TO FINALLY ACCEPT THAT NOTHING THAT COULD HAPPEN DEPENDED ON ME.

THAT NIGHT WE SLEPT AT THE HOUSE OF SOME ANA'S FRIENDS.

DID SOMETHING HAPPEN?

I DON'T KNOW. I GOT DIZZY WHEN I RETURNED FROM THE BATHROOM.

BUT ARE YOU OK?

I DON'T THINK SO. MY HEART'S ACTING FUNNY. I HAVE ARRHYTHMIA.

I THINK I'M GOING TO DIE.

COME ON, DON'T BE SILLY.

I'M GOING TO GET YOU A GLASS OF WATER.

THAT'S IT, I THOUGHT WITH THE UTMOST NATURALNESS.

THAT'S IT.

AWAKENING IS LITERALLY BEYOND THE MIND, BEYOND ANYTHING THAT YOU CAN THINK OR IMAGINE, BUT AT THE SAME TIME YOU RECOGNIZE IT AS SOMETHING FAMILIAR, SOMETHING ABSOLUTELY INTIMATE: YOUR TRUE BEING.

WITH ONE IMPORTANT REMARK, AND IS THAT "YOU" ARE NOT THERE. NOBODY EVER AWAKENED TO CONSCIOUSNESS, BUT RATHER THE CONTRARY. IT IS CONSCIOUSNESS WHICH AWAKENS FROM THE IDENTIFICATION WITH THE PERSON: IT AWAKES TO ITSELF BY ITSELF.

106

CHAPTER THREE

"(DRINK DRINK)"

WHY HAVE YOU WANTED TO SO URGENTLY SEE ME, APPRENTICE?

I WANTED TO SEE YOU, REVERED TEACHER, BECAUSE YESTERDAY WHILE MEDITATING I REACHED SATORI.

SATORI? HAVE YOU REALLY COME TO BOTHER ME ABOUT THIS? YOU DO NOT HAVE THE SLIGHTEST IDEA OF WHAT SATORI IS...

NOW LEAVE.

ONE YEAR LATER

MAY I KNOW WHAT IT IS YOU WANT NOW?

TEACHER, SINCERELY, I DO BELIEVE THAT IT WAS SATORI.

ONCE AGAIN, THIS?

LEAVE MY SIGHT AND GO MEDITATE. PERHAPS IN THIS WAY YOU SHALL REACH SATORI.

PARDON ME, TEACHER.

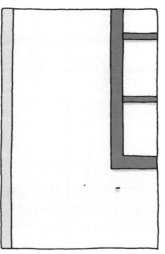

112

ANA WASN'T DOING SO WELL FINANCIALLY, AND I WAS GOING TO BE OUT TRAVELING FOR ALMOST THREE MONTHS, SO WE DIDN'T HAVE MUCH REASON TO KEEP THE APARTMENT. WE PAID NOVEMBER RENT AND LEFT.

FURTHERMORE, A FEW WEEKS PRIOR TO MY DEPARTURE WE HAD ONE OF THOSE BIG FIGHTS.

WE DECIDED TO GIVE OURSELVES TIME TO RETHINK THE RELATIONSHIP WHILE I WAS AWAY.

TO TOP IT ALL OF, IT COINCIDED WITH A BAD STREAK HER FATHER WAS GOING THROUGH: HE WAS DIAGNOSED WITH DEPRESSION.

NEVERTHELESS WE DECIDED TO GIVE EACH OTHER SPACE. NO LETTERS, NO PHONE CALLS, NO E-MAILS. NOTHING.

I ARRIVED IN INDIA AT THE BEGINNING OF NOVEMBER. MOST OF ALL I WANTED TO VISIT RISHIKESH AS WELL AS THIRUVANNAMALAI, WHICH IS A SMALL CITY IN TAMIL NADU, AT THE SOUTHERNMOST PART OF THE SUBCONTINENT.

SINCE THEY WERE AT OPPOSITE ENDS (2000 KM) I HAD NO CHOICE BUT TO SPEND ENTIRE DAYS TRAVELING ON TRAINS, BUSES, ETC.

BEEP

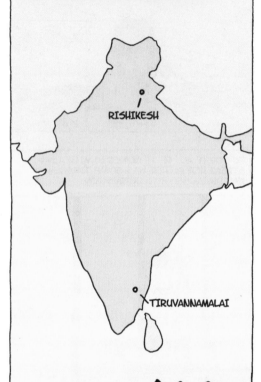

RISHIKESH

TIRUVANNAMALAI

VERI KOLAVERI.?.

AFTER MORE THAN 40 HOURS TRAVELING FROM VARANASI TO CHENNAI, A BUS DROPPED ME OFF IN THIRUVANNAMALAI (IT TOOK ONLY 6 HOURS!).

THIRUVANNAMALAI IS A HAPPENING
PILGRIM DESTINATION IN TAMIL NADU.

IT'S TEMPLE, DEVOTED TO THE FIRE
ELEMENT, IS ONE OF THE MOST SACRED
PLACES FOR THE DEVOTEES OF SHIVA,
AND THE MOUNTAIN WHICH LOOMS OVER
THE CITY, ARUNACHALA, IS VENERATED
AS AN MANIFESTATION OF THE DIVINITY.

FOR WESTERNERS
THIRUVANNAMALAI IS KNOWN
MAINLY DUE TO THE FIGURE
OF RAMANA MAHARSHI.

THE TEACHER WHO TAUGHT
THROUGH SILENCE.

117

SRI BHAGAVAN RAMANA MAHARSHI (1879-1950) WAS ONE OF THE KEY FIGURES OF INDIAN SPIRITUAL LIFE IN THE TWENTIETH CENTURY, AND IS AN ESSENTIAL REFERENCE IN THE CURRENT ADVAITA VEDANTA TEACHING, IN SPITE OF THE FACT THAT, STRICTLY SPEAKING, HE NEVER BELONGED TO ANY RELIGIOUS OR SPIRITUAL SCHOOL.

AT THE AGE OF SIXTEEN SRI BHAGAVAN EXPERIENCED WHAT HE WOULD LATER DESCRIBE AS LIBERATION (MUKTI), AND SHORTLY AFTER LEFT THE HOUSE IN WHICH HE LIVED WITH HIS UNCLE IN ORDER TO TRAVEL TO THIRUVANNAMALAI (WHICH, EVEN THEN, WAS A POPULAR PILGRIMAGE DESTINATION FOR HINDUS) TO PERSONALLY SEE WHAT HE HAD ALWAYS CONSIDERED TO BE HIS GURU: ARUNACHALA, THE HOLY MOUNTAIN.

HE GOT RID OF HIS MONEY, HIS CLOTHES, AND HIS CASTE TRAPPINGS AND FOR THE REST OF HIS LIFE NEVER ONCE MOVED FROM THAT PLACE.

WITH THE PASSAGE OF TIME, INCREASING NUMBERS OF PEOPLE CAME TO SEE HIM, DESIROUS TO EXPLAIN HIM THEIR DOUBTS REGARDING THE PATH TO LIBERATION OR SIMPLY TO ENJOY HIS COMPANY IN SILENCE -DURING HIS FIRST FEW YEARS IN THE CITY HE DIDN'T SPEAK A WORD. HE HAD THOUSANDS OF FOLLOWERS AND AN ASHRAM WAS FORMED AT THE FOOT OF THE MOUNTAIN -THE RAMANASHRAM- SO THAT WHOEVER WANTED TO COULD SPEND SOME TIME IN THE VICINITY OF THE SAGE. TODAY THIS ASHRAM HOSTS AN INCESSANT FLOW OF SEEKERS FROM ALL WALKS OF LIFE.

RAMANA ALWAYS CLAIMED THAT ARUNACHALA WAS THE SPIRITUAL HEART OF THE WORLD.

"THIRU" IS FULL OF TEACHERS AND GURUS, BUT THE TRUTH IS THAT THE TYPE OF SPIRITUAL MARKETPLACE I FOUND MYSELF IN WASN'T MUCH TO MY LIKING.

VANAKAM!

VANAKAM!*

* THE TAMIL GREETING

THE AFFECTED POSING OF SOME SEEKERS AND THE "DISTANCE" SOME TEACHERS IMPOSED WASN'T MY CUP OF TEA.

AND SO IN THE END, I CHOSE TO FORGET ABOUT FINDING ANOTHER GUIDE APART FROM RAMANA MAHARSHI'S BOOKS AND SET ABOUT ENJOYING THE INVITING ATMOSPHERE OF THE ASHRAM AND ITS SURROUNDINGS.

DURING MY LAST TWO DAYS IN THIRU I STAYED IN THE RAMANASHRAM. THE SEARCH FOR A TEACHER APPEARED RELEGATED TO SOME SORT OF LIMBO, BUT ONE CAN ALWAYS LEARN THINGS. IT WAS THERE THAT I LEARNED A BEAUTIFUL LESSON.

I LEARNED TO APPRECIATE THE VALUE OF DEVOTION.

I HAD ALWAYS THOUGHT THAT SHOWINGS OF DEVOTION WERE SIGNS OF IRRATIONALITY AND FANATICISM, BUT THERE I BECAME AWARE THAT THIS DIDN'T ALWAYS HAVE TO BE THE CASE.

IT'S TRUE THAT IN SOME RELIGIONS AND SPIRITUAL MOVEMENTS THERE ARE CERTAIN COMPONENTS RELATED TO DEVOTIONAL PRACTICES THAT ARE SLIGHTLY UNHEALTHY.

BUT THIS DOESN'T CHANGE THE FACT THAT FOR MANY THESE ACTS ARE STILL EXPRESSIONS OF LOVE, RESPECT, AND HUMILITY PERFECTLY VALID.

WHAT ARE YOU WORKING ON NOW?

I'M WRESTLING WITH THE THIRD CHAPTER OF THE COMIC.

AH!

SO, IT HAS MORE CHAPTERS?

YES, THERE ARE IN FACT THREE. THIS WOULD BE THE LAST ONE.

I THOUGHT IT ENDED THERE.

ACTUALLY THE SAME THING HAPPENED TO ANA. WHEN SHE READ EARLY VERSIONS OF THE SCRIPT, SHE THOUGHT THE STORY ENDED THERE, BUT NO, IT DOESN'T, IT KEEPS GOING A BIT MORE.

IN FACT, I'M PROBABLY STUMPED FOR THIS REASON. THE THIRD PART IS NECESSARY, BUT AFTER THE WAY IN WHICH THE SECOND ENDS I DON'T KNOW IF I'LL BE ABLE TO KEEP IT INTERESTING. I'M NOT TOO SURE...

I HEAR YOU. IT CAN'T BE EASY.

IF YOU WANT, I'LL SEND IT TO YOU WHEN IS FINISHED AND YOU CAN TELL ME WHAT YOU THINK.

RIGHT ON!

After the grueling trip to Chennai, on the trip back I decided to take my time a bit more: instead of two days I took two weeks to get to the Himalayan foothills.

What's that?

We were just saying that you look like Sai Baba.

Shirdi Sai Baba.

You're the spitting image.

Only you got dark hair.

Shirdi Sai Baba

Me imitating Sai Baba

* TEA, HOT TEA

127

SO YOU'RE NOT LOOKING FOR A TEACHER.

HERE IN RISHIKESH EVERYONE IS LOOKING FOR A TEACHER!

I SUPPOSE I AM, BUT NOT THE TYPE THAT HANGS OUT IN THESE SORTS OF PLACES.

I'M LOOKING FOR SOMEONE WHO HAS ALREADY WALKED THE PATH AND WHO CAN GIVE ME ADVICE.

I DON'T KNOW.

SOMEONE WHO I CAN TALK OPENLY ABOUT ALL THIS WITH.

A FRIEND, I GUESS.

128

I RECALL THAT IN THOSE FINAL DAYS IN INDIA I THOUGHT OFTEN ABOUT THE MEANING OF WHAT HAD HAPPENED THAT NIGHT IN OURENSE. ON THE ONE HAND I KNEW WHAT IT WAS AND WHAT IT MEANT, BUT ON THE OTHER HAND IT WAS AS IF I WASN'T ABLE TO ACCEPT IT.

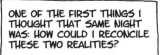

ONE OF THE FIRST THINGS I THOUGHT THAT SAME NIGHT WAS: HOW COULD I RECONCILE THESE TWO REALITIES?

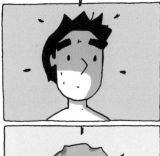

HOW COULD I RECONCILE THAT "REVELATION" WITH THIS LIFE?

GRRR...

GET OUT OF MY ROOM IMMEDIATELY!

GRRR

AND DON'T EVEN THINK ABOUT COMING BACK...

IF THE FIRST PHASE FOR THE MYSTICS WAS THE PURGATIVE WAY, AND THIS IS THEN FOLLOWED BY ENLIGHTENMENT, THE THIRD IS UNION.

ALTHOUGH FOR MANY TRADITIONS THE END OF THE ROAD IS ENLIGHTENMENT, OTHERS SUCH AS ZEN INSIST THAT UPON AWAKENING THERE IS STILL THE TASK OF ESTABLISHING ONESELF IN KNOWLEDGE: A TASK WHICH IS AS IMPORTANT, OR EVEN MORE SO, THAN THE FIRST.

THERE IS A COMMON BELIEF SURROUNDING THE AWAKENING: MANY PEOPLE THINK THAT HE OR SHE WHO AWAKES SUDDENLY BECOMES AN OMNISCIENT AND POWERFUL SAGE. A SUPERMAN OF SORTS. THE REALITY, IN MOST CASES, IS A FAR CRY FROM THIS IMAGE. IN FACT, THE INITIAL MOMENTS IN THE DISCOVERY OF OUR TRUE NATURE CAN BE QUITE DESTABILIZING, AND WHILE THINGS ARE STILL UNSETTLED THERE IS A SORT OF BACK AND FORTH MOVEMENT BETWEEN WHAT YOU NOW KNOW AND WHAT YOUR OLD HABITS (BODILY, MENTAL, EMOTIONAL...) TELL YOU.

IN SOME SENSE EVERYTHING ENDS UPON AWAKENING. WHILE THIS MAY BE TRUE, IN ANOTHER SENSE, ONE THAT'S PERHAPS MORE INTERESTING AND RICHER, THERE IS STILL PLENTY OF ROAD AHEAD.

2012

I STAYED AT THE APARTMENT OF A FRIEND, IN SANTIAGO, WHILE LOOKING FOR A PLACE, EVEN THOUGH I WASN'T REALLY SURE IF I WANTED TO STAY IN THE CITY.

I WAS ALRIGHT, ALTHOUGH HONESTLY I WAS STARTING TO FEEL AT EASY ANYWHERE.

IN FACT, I WAS COMFORTABLE IN ANY PLACE OR CIRCUMSTANCE.

ANA AND I HAD BROKEN UP, I DIDN'T HAVE A HOUSE, NOR DID I HAVE ANY INTENTION TO WORK THAT YEAR.

AFTERNOON!

HOW'S IT GOING, INDIAN!?

AND THE TRUTH WAS I DIDN'T CARE: I WAS IN A GOOD PLACE. I DON'T THINK I HAD EVER FELT SO FREE FROM WORRY.

HOWEVER MY ATTITUDE WAS INTERPRETED BY THOSE AROUND ME AS RATHER RECKLESS.

ARE YOU POSITIVE YOU'RE NOT GOING TO GO BACK TO WORK?

POSITIVE. I'M GOING TO RETIRE.

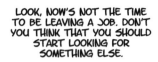

LOOK, NOW'S NOT THE TIME TO BE LEAVING A JOB. DON'T YOU THINK THAT YOU SHOULD START LOOKING FOR SOMETHING ELSE.

LIKE WHAT?

I DON'T KNOW. ANYTHING. YOU CAN'T JUST BE LIKE THIS, MATE.

WHY NOT? HAVE YOU EVER TRIED IT?

IT WORKS PRETTY WELL FOR ME.

THAT'S NOT TRUE. NOBODY IS GOOD LIKE THIS: AT THE MERCY OF FATE. BUT IF YOU WANT TO FOOL YOURSELF, GO RIGHT AHEAD!

GULP!

LEAVING BEHIND WORRY AND STRESS OVER THE FUTURE OR THE OPINIONS OF OTHERS DOESN'T MAKE YOU A SLACKER, AND, IN NO WAY CORRESPONDS TO A BLASÉ ATTITUDE OR IMPLIES A LACK OF ETHICS.

THE OPPOSITE IS IN FACT TRUE: IT'S ONLY WHEN YOU STOP PAYING ATTENTION TO THESE FALSE PROBLEMS THAT YOU BECOME FREE TO ACT ACCORDING TO YOUR TASTES AND PERSONALITY WITHOUT HAVING YOUR ACTIONS COLORED BY THE NEED TO MAINTAIN A PARTICULAR SELF-IMAGE OR TO FULFILL EXPECTATIONS.

FOR EXAMPLE, NOW I COULD SEE ME TAKING INITIATIVES THAT YEARS AGO I WOULD HAVE DISCARDED OUT OF PRIDE, OR WOULD HAVE ACCEPTED WITH RESERVATIONS.

BEEP
BUP
BUP
BEEP

HEY! HOW'S IT GOING?

DO YOU HAVE A MOMENT TO TALK?

I'VE BEEN THINKING ABOUT OUR CONVERSATION THE OTHER DAY, AND I THINK I OWE YOU AND APOLOGY...

I FOUND A ROOM IN A SHARED FLAT IN THE OLD PART OF TOWN. IT WAS BIG, CENTRAL, AND INEXPENSIVE.

YOUR ROOMMATES ARE QUITE NICE.

MY MAIN CONCERN WAS IN PAINTING WATERCOLORS FOR A FRIEND'S SHOP.

YEAH, IN THAT SENSE I GOT LUCKY.

AT ANY RATE, I WAS WONDERING... WHAT IF I WERE TO LIVE WITH YOU AND YOUR FATHER IN YOUR HOUSE IN THE COUNTRY.

HMMM... I DON'T THINK SO.

IT SEEMS TO ME THAT YOU DON'T KNOW WHAT TO DO WITH YOUR LIFE AND YOU JUST WANT TO JUMP ON BOARD.

DID YOU KNOW THAT YOU'RE VERY UNPLEASANT AT TIMES?

139

IF DURING THE FIRST PART OF THIS ADVENTURE IT'S YOU THAT SEEKS OUT THE TRUTH, AFTER THE MOMENT OF RECOGNITION, IT IS THE TRUTH THAT SEEKS YOU OUT.

AT THE MOST UNEXPECTED MOMENTS I WAS SURPRISED BY "THE REAL" WITH A FORCE WHICH WAS BOTH BRUTAL AND SUBTLE AT THE SAME TIME. IT WAS, IN FACT, ALMOST IMPERCEPTIBLE.

DESPITE BEING THE CLOSEST AND MOST INTIMATE TO US IT IS INDESCRIBABLE. IT ESCAPES US. "THE REAL" IS PRESENT ALWAYS AND IN EVERY CIRCUMSTANCE. NEVERTHELESS WE SPEND OUR LIVE IGNORING IT, UNABLE TO EVEN SEE IT.

AT THESE TIMES I REALIZED, WITH AN OVERWHELMING CLARITY, THAT THE SOLUTION TO THE WHOLE SEARCH THING HAD BEEN ALWAYS RIGHT IN FRONT OF ME.

IT IS SOMETHING LIKE WHEN YOU GET TIRED OF TRYING TO FIND A SOLUTION TO A PROBLEM THAT'S BEEN BOTHERING YOU FOR SOME TIME: IT'S ONLY WHEN YOU'VE GIVEN UP THE HOPE OF FINDING A SOLUTION THAT THE ANSWER SEEMS TO REVEAL ITSELF ON ITS OWN, AS IF BY CHANCE, AND IT STRIKES YOU AS SO SIMPLE AND OBVIOUS THAT YOU FEEL LIKE LAUGHING AT THE ABSURDITY OF THE SITUATION.

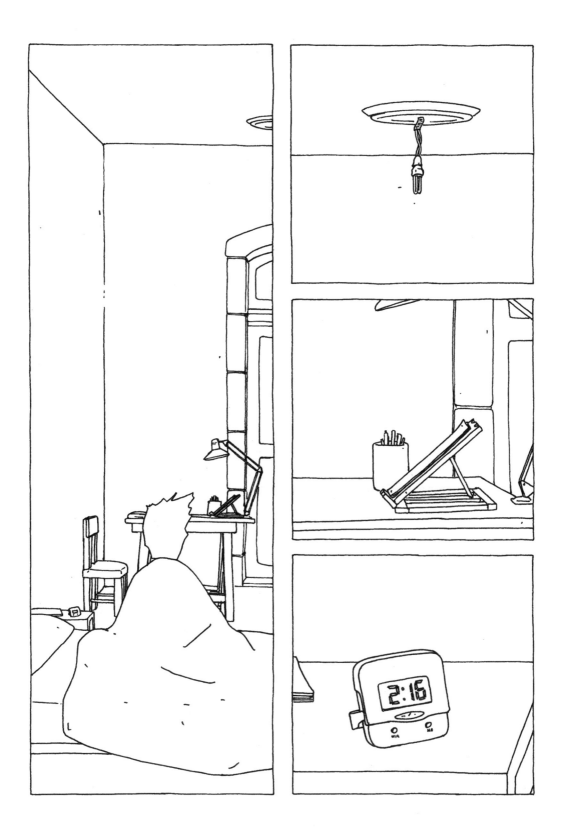

SO YOU FINISHED IT ALL?

WELL, I HAVE TO MAKE SOME CORRECTIONS AND CHANGE THINGS HERE AND THERE, MAYBE EVEN ADD A PAGE OR TWO, BUT YES: AS FAR AS THE CORE STORY IS CONCERNED WE CAN SAY IS FINISHED.

AND WHEN CAN I SEE IT?

AS SOON AS YOU HAVE THE TIME TO TAKE A LOOK AT IT.

COOL. AND AS SOON AS I READ IT I START WRITING MY OWN ACCOUNT OF THE FACTS. I'M GONNA MAKE A BOOK, A COMIC BOOK PERHAPS.

I BEG YOUR PARDON...

WHAT!? I HAVE MY OWN VIEW ABOUT IT ALL AND THE RIGHT TO TELL IT TOO. WHAT OF IT?

RIGHT...

AND WHAT ARE YOU GONNA CALL THAT? "THE TRUE STORY"?

HA HA HA

MAYBE... DO YOU HAVE ANY PROBLEM WITH THAT?

ON THE CONTRARY: I CAN'T WAIT TO SEE IT...

BRRRRR

THE PROCESS SEEMED TO BE FOLLOWING ITS COURSE, REGARDLESS OF ANY EXTERNAL CIRCUMSTANCES.

HELPING OUT ANA AND HER COLLEAGUE SUSANA WITH A RESTORATION PROJECT

THROUGHOUT THOSE FIRST MONTHS I COULD SEE HOW THE RESISTANCE THAT I HAD PUT UP AGAINST IT ALL BEGAN TO FALL ONE AFTER ANOTHER, LIKE DOMINO PIECES.

BUT I CONTINUED TO HAVE THE OCCASIONAL MOMENTS OF DOUBT AND AGITATION. I DECIDED THAT IT WOULD BE A GOOD IDEA TO SEEK OUT SOME "PROFESSIONAL ADVICE."

SO I HEAR YOU'RE GOING TO BARCELONA THIS WEEKEND.

THAT'S RIGHT. IT'S A KIND OF RETREAT. MEDITATION AND THESE SORTS OF THINGS, YOU KNOW...

I DON'T GIVE SPEECHES, SO IF SOMEONE HAS ANY QUESTION...

THERE IS A DEEPENING OF THE EXPERIENCE AFTER A GLIMPSE OF THE TRUTH. OVER TIME, THAT WHICH HAS BEEN UNDERSTOOD PERMEATES EVERY LEVEL OF THE BODY AND THE MIND.

THERE IS A PROCESS THROUGH WHICH THE BODY-MIND REALIGNS ITSELF WITH THE TRUTH IF YOU LIVE HARMONIOUSLY INSIDE.

...AT SOME POINT THE PROBLEMS AND MISERY VANISH. BUT THE ADVENTURE AND THE BEAUTY CONTINUE.

ANY RESIDUAL SUFFERING OR FEELING OF INADEQUACY SIMPLY REFLECTS THE PERSISTENCE OF OLD HABITS. WHAT COUNTS IS NOT AN EXPERIENCE WE HAVE OF AWAKENING, AN EXPERIENCE THAT MAY BE EXCITING AT THE TIME BUT WHICH EVENTUALLY FADES AWAY AND LEAVE US DISSATISFIED.

WHAT COUNTS IS THE PERMANENT SATISFACTION IN WHICH WE LIVE AS A RESULT OF OUR HAVING RECOGNIZED WHAT WE TRULY ARE.

SO YOU LEARNED ABOUT FRANCIS* THROUGH THE WEBPAGE?

YES. BY CHANCE. LOOKING FOR SOMETHING ELSE, I WOUND UP THERE.

IT'S REALLY WELL DONE.

* FRANCIS LUCILLE.

THANKS. I'M GLAD IT TURNED OUT TO BE USEFUL TO SOMEONE BECAUSE TO TELL THE TRUTH IT HASN'T BEEN TOO SUCCESSFUL WITH THE STUDENTS OF THE YOGA ACADEMY.

THESE SUBJECTS AREN'T THAT ALLURING.

YOU'D BE SURPRISED. NOT EVEN THE TEACHERS THEMSELVES ARE INTERESTED IN THEM.

REALLY?

REALLY! THE MAJORITY TEACH YOGA AS IF IT WERE A SORT OF GYMNASTICS OR SOMETHING, WHILE THE FOUNDATION, WHAT IS ESSENTIALLY IMPORTANT, IS LEFT OUT.

SO YOU'RE SAYING THAT NOT EVEN THE PROFESSIONALS IN THE FIELD ARE INTERESTED IN THE SUBJECT.

WELL... MAYBE WE ARE INDEED "WEIRDOS."

AT THE RETREAT I MET PEDRO, ANOTHER TEACHER, AND IT TURNED OUT THAT HE LIVED FIVE MINUTES WALKING DISTANCE FROM MY PARENTS' HOUSE. WE EXCHANGED PHONE NUMBERS AND SOME TIME LATER I PAID HIM A VISIT.

AT THAT MEETING PEDRO DIDN'T SAY ANYTHING SPECIAL OR ANYTHING THAT I HADN'T HEARD BEFORE, NEVERTHELESS THE MEETING WAS EXTREMELY IMPORTANT.

PERHAPS IT WAS SEEING HOW A PERSON WHO HAD GONE THROUGH THE ENTIRE ORDEAL COULD CARRY ON A NORMAL LIFE, SIMPLY, OR MAYBE IT WAS THE FACT THAT SOMEONE COULD LISTEN TO WHAT I WAS SAYING FROM A PEACEFUL PLACE, WHICH IN TURN CALMED ME... WHATEVER THE CASE THAT SHORT CONVERSATION WAS A LANDMARK MOMENT IN THE ENTIRE PROCESS.

IN THE FOLLOWING WEEKS THOSE MOMENTS WHICH REALITY WOULD SURPRISE ME AND EVERYTHING BECOME CLEAR AND SIMPLE WENT FROM BEING ANECDOTES TO BEING THE NORM: OVER TIME THE EXTRAORDINARY SETTLED OVER MY DAY TO DAY LIFE, AND ONLY VERY OCCASIONALLY, BY LOOKING BACK, COULD I APPRECIATE THE REMARKABLE CHANGE THAT WAS TAKING PLACE.

IT WAS TRUE THAT FROM TIME TO TIME I WAS STILL GRIPPED BY DOUBT AND UNEASE, BUT IT WAS INCREASINGLY LESS COMMON AND LESS PENETRATING, AND AS IT BECAME MORE SPORADIC AND SPREAD OUT OVER TIME, PEACE AND TRANQUILITY BEGAN TO OCCUPY THOSE VACANT SPACES.

AND AFTER WHAT HAPPENED TO YOU AND ALL OF THESE THINGS YOU'RE LEARNING, AREN'T YOU AFRAID THAT YOU'LL START THINKING YOU'RE BETTER THAN EVERYONE ELSE?

I SUPPOSE THAT DANGER EXISTS, BUT FOR THIS AND OTHER REASONS, WE HAVE TEACHERS...

FOR PLACING EXPERIENCE IN ITS PROPER PERSPECTIVE...

AND FOR...

WE HAVE TO GET OUT OF THE WAY SWEETHEART.

AT THE BEGINNING OF OCTOBER, BEFORE ANA BEGAN THE TERM, I MOVED.

WITHOUT KNOWING HOW TO DRIVE AND WITH NO BUS SERVICE NEARBY, I WAS CERTAINLY QUITE REMOVED (THOUGH THIS DIDN'T SEEM TO ME TO BE MUCH OF A PROBLEM). IN EVERY OTHER ASPECT THE PLACE WAS PERFECT: I HAD LAND FOR LONG WALKS, WHICH IS WHAT I LIKE, AND PLENTY OF FREE TIME.

THE REALITY IS THAT IT WAS THE BEST SOLUTION FOR EVERYONE, EVEN FOR YOLA, WHO WAS OLD AND NEEDED MORE AND MORE CARE EVERY DAY.

ONE YEAR AFTER

FOR SOME TIME I WAS WAITING, OR AT LEAST I WAS CURIOUS, ABOUT HOW EVERYTHING WOULD TURN OUT, UNTIL I REALIZED THAT THIS WAITING DIDN'T MAKE ANY SENSE.

REALITY HAD ALWAYS BEEN THERE, AND IT HAD
ALWAYS BEEN IN FULL SIGHT. THERE HAD NEVER
BEEN A MOMENT THAT IT HADN'T BEEN, AND
THERE WOULD NEVER BE A MOMENT WHEN IT
WOULD CHANGE INTO SOMETHING DIFFERENT,
INTO SOMETHING BETTER OR MORE COMPLETE.

NO EVENT OR EXPERIENCE, NO PROCESS, COULD
MAKE REALITY MORE REAL THAN IT ALREADY WAS.

WAITING FOR "THE END OF THE PROCESS" WAS
NOTHING MORE THAN ANOTHER TRICK, ANOTHER
MANIFESTATION, IN A NEW DISGUISE, OF THE
FEELING OF LACK.

YOU
CAN COME
NOW!

THINGS DON'T BEGIN TO MAKE SENSE WHEN EACH AND EVERY QUESTION IS ANSWERED, CATALOGUED, AND CLOSED OFF, BUT RATHER WHEN THESE LOSE THEIR URGENCY AND YOU CAN LIVE IN OPENNESS.

THIS JOURNEY DOESN'T TAKE YOU TO ANY NEW OR DIFFERENT PLACE. INSTEAD, IT BRINGS YOU TO RECOGNIZE AND APPRECIATE WHAT HAS ALWAYS BEEN THERE, THE BACKDROP OF PEACE AND TRANQUILITY WHERE THE LIFE PLAYS ITSELF OUT, AND WHICH IS AND ALWAYS WAS PRESENT, EVEN WHEN THINGS DIN'T SEEM TO BE GOING SO WELL.

159

END

THANKS TO ANA FOR HER COUNSEL, HER SUPPORT AND HER PA-
TIENCE THROUGH ALL THIS YEARS.

THIS COMIC TOOK BENEFIT IN CRUCIAL WAYS FROM THE ADVICE AND
COUNSEL OF CIBRAN.

THANKS TOO TO MARK FOR DOING HIS PART SO QUICK AND SO
WELL.

I AM GRATEFUL TO FRANCIS FOR HIS GENEROSITY AND FOR HIS
WONDERFUL TEACHINGS.

I AM INDEBTED TO EVA, JOSE, SUSANA AND PEDRO FOR THEIR HELP,
COUNSEL AND ENTHUSIASM.

I WOULD LIKE TO THANK TOO SADRA, PAUL, PAULO AND ESTHER,
CARME, ALMU, ALI AND VICTOR, XAIME LIS, CAMINO, DAVID ORIHUELA,
DAVID AMBOAGE, MARIANO, FRAN AND CANDIDO, MARIANA, IRIA, TANTI,
ANA COLOMBIA, SWAMI MUKTANANDA, THE NUNS AT SUAN MOKK AND
ALL THE PEOPLE WHO HELPED ME ONE WAY OR ANOTHER ALONG THE
PROCESS OF CREATING THIS BOOK.

SPECIAL THANKS ARE OWED TO MY FAMILY AND FRIENDS!

AND LAST BUT NOT LEAST THANKS TO CATHERINE AND JULIAN FOR
TRUSTING THE PROJECT FROM THE MOMENT THEY SAW IT AND FOR
THE GREAT WORK THEY ARE DOING AT NON-DUALITY PRESS.

THANK YOU ALL,

IVAN

Iván Sende studied illustration at the School of Arts Pablo Picasso. His first published book as illustrator was *Usha* (Xerais, 2008), which was followed by *Lía e as Zapatillas de Deportes* (Xerais, 2008), O *Monstro das Palabras* (Xerais, 2009), and *Volvo!* O *Regreso de Usha* (Xerais, 2014), all of them written by the Galician author, Maria Reimóndez.

  Bea (Xerais, 2008) was his first book as author in his own right and he was later shortlisted for the Merlín award – one of the more important prizes for children's writers – with *Carabranca*, which was self-published in 2011.

  In 2015 he illustrated *SIRA e o ROBOT: Adventures on Titan* (Xerais), a CD-book by Mark Wiersma and Miguel Mosqueira.

ADVAITA: THE COMIC
First edition published September 2015 by Non-Duality Press
©Iván Sende 2015
Translated from Galician by Mark Wiersma

Non-Duality Press
An imprint of New Harbinger Publications

ISBN: 978-1-908664-54-9   Printed in Canada